My Greek Family Table

My Greek Family Table

Τὸ Ελληνικό οικογενειακό τραπέζι μου

Maria Benardis

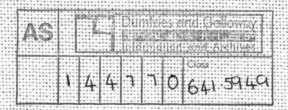
Photography by Alan Benson

LANTERN
an imprint of
PENGUIN BOOKS

I dedicate this book to the memory of my
mother, Ioanna. Her spirit guides me as
I pursue my passion for food.

Contents

Introduction

Growing up in a Greek household, first on a small Greek island and then in Australia, meant that I was constantly surrounded by family, friends and food. There was always some cultural or religious occasion, such as a wedding, christening or name day, to celebrate. Each invited guest would bring a dish, either sweet or savoury. At these festivities I would spend most of my time near the kitchen so that I could see each special dish being unveiled. I was always amazed by the care each guest had taken to present the food in a visually spectacular way.

The women would gather in one room and converse on many subjects, but food was always top of the agenda. They would reminisce about Greece and exchange memories, both happy and sad. When food was discussed each dish would have a story attached to it. It was during these gatherings that I began to develop a deeper understanding and appreciation for these women and for Greek cuisine. I have included some of their stories in this book, as many of them are so intricately associated with dishes I grew up eating and still cook today.

Because eating at a Greek table is as much about ritual as it is about sustenance, before the meal there is always a blessing of the food, followed by the words *Kalli orexi* and *Stin igia sas* ('Good appetite' and 'To your health'). And it wouldn't be a Greek meal without a toast with wine or *ouzo*.

In Greek cooking today, the influence of the ancients is still evident. Many of the same ingredients that the ancient Greeks prized are central to modern Greek cooking. Ingredients are handled with respect and presented with care, just as they were all those millennia ago. Perhaps the reason Greeks today treat the act of sharing food with often religious and philosophical significance comes from their roots. In ancient times Greeks never ate meat unless it had been sacrificed to a god, and certain vegetables were considered 'cleaner' than others.

Much of the food prepared on the mainland by the ancient Greeks was relatively simple and minimally spiced. The concept of sweet and sour – such as vinegar or *garos* (fish sauce) combined with honey – was of great importance. Archestratus, renowned as the father of gastronomy and the writer of the first cookbook, took great care to follow this philosophy so as best to enhance the overall harmony of tastes and aromas.

The resulting Greek cuisine has been influencing the culinary traditions of other cultures for thousands of years. Many recipes with Turkish names have their origins in Greek cooking. The Romans also adopted and imitated Greek dishes, ingredients and cooking styles after employing Athenian cooks and later procuring the services of Greek tutors for the education of their children. This ultimately resulted in Greek cuisine influencing some of the Italian and French culinary traditions.

Greece's more modern history has also made a deep impression on the way that Greek people eat. The Second World War was a time of great deprivation and many people had to be inventive with the dishes they cooked, simply in order to survive. In the years that followed, many – my family included – left their homeland to begin new lives in Australia. As well as suitcases filled with their beloved ingredients, they brought with them a notion central to Greek cuisine: *kerasma*, the sharing and offering of food to loved ones.

This book is as much about the importance of the family and friends who share our table as it is about food. I include here stories from my own family – about what it is that makes them so uniquely Greek and how I have come to honour my Greek heritage. My mother's side of the family has had the strongest influence on me when it comes to food. When I cook I sense their spirit and energy guiding me to produce dishes that capture cultural traditions and family secrets.

Greek people are passionate about their food; they blossom like flowers when they are around it. They are so proud of their cuisine that the Greek postal office often releases postage stamps to showcase dishes and to share recipes with the rest of the world. And I am no exception!

When you try these recipes, I hope you'll feel the same connection with Greece that I do.

A puppet from the Greek shadow theatre, which is popular entertainment for children and adults alike. This character's name is Karakiozis.

Salads

At the Greek table, a salad is always served at the start of the meal, followed by the *meze*. Each region of Greece has a signature salad designed to capitalise on locally grown ingredients, such as tomatoes, beetroot, cucumbers, olives, pulses, anchovies, capers, caper leaves, rusks, fresh herbs, pomegranates and wild greens. They also feature locally made products such as olive oil, red wine vinegar, a variety of cheeses and cured meats and sausages. Some dips on the *meze* table, such as *taramosalata*, are also called salads. The components of each salad are so fresh and vibrant that the ingredients list is generally kept fairly short, giving each flavour the opportunity to shine.

Traditional Kalamata salad

The traditional Kalamata salad, known in Greece as *'horiatiki salata'* (or villagers' salad) when other ingredients such as capsicum or purslane are added, comprises Kalamata olives, tomatoes, cucumber, Greek feta and onion. Many people incorrectly call it a 'Greek' salad and add other ingredients; however, I prefer the traditional blend and do not alter the quantities or compromise on the quality of the ingredients. I don't tend to add red wine vinegar to the salad, but you can if you like.

The word *feta* means 'slice'. Most eateries in Greece therefore slice the feta rather than cut it into cubes, and place it on top of the salad just before serving.

4 large ripe tomatoes
1 Lebanese cucumber
1 large red onion
18 Kalamata olives
150 g Greek feta, in one
   thin slice
sea salt
dried wild oregano, to taste
extra virgin olive oil,
   for drizzling

Serves 4

Wash and dry the tomatoes and cucumber. Cut the tomatoes into quarters. Cut the cucumber into thin rounds.

Peel the onion and slice into thin rounds.

Combine the tomato, cucumber, onion and olives in a large bowl and balance the piece of feta on top.

Sprinkle sea salt and oregano over the salad to taste, and drizzle with extra virgin olive oil just before serving.

Fresh broad bean and dill salad

This simple salad can be eaten on its own or as a side dish. I sometimes add artichokes for something different or crumble feta over the top.

1 kg fresh broad beans
2 tablespoons olive oil
juice of 1 lemon
½ teaspoon grated lemon zest
sea salt and cracked pepper
3 tablespoons chopped dill

Serves 4

Shell the broad beans, then place in a saucepan of salted water and simmer over low heat for about 15 minutes. Drain. Remove the outer skin by pinching it, then push the bean out.

Place the beans in a bowl and add the olive oil, lemon juice and zest, salt and pepper. Toss gently, then add the dill and toss again.

Barley and pomegranate salad >

This recipe was inspired by a dish eaten in ancient times made with crushed wheat, cheese, honey, pomegranate and nuts. Before serving, I often spoon the salad into moulds and turn them onto serving plates. You can eat this on its own or as a side dish.

250 g pearl barley
200 g Greek feta
½ cup pomegranate seeds,
   plus extra to garnish
50 g walnuts, toasted and
   roughly chopped
3 tablespoons finely chopped
   mint, plus extra leaves
   to garnish
2 tablespoons finely chopped
   flat-leaf parsley, plus extra
   leaves to garnish
3 tablespoons finely chopped
   spring onion

Dressing
2 teaspoons ground cumin
3 tablespoons olive oil
2 tablespoons red wine
   vinegar
1 tablespoon honey
1–2 cloves garlic, crushed
sea salt and cracked pepper

Serves 4

Bring 3 cups of salted water to the boil, then reduce to a simmer. Rinse the pearl barley and add to the pan. Cook for 20–25 minutes or until the barley has softened. Drain, then place in a bowl and cool to room temperature.

Cut the feta into cubes and add to the barley with the remaining salad ingredients. Mix together well.

Combine the dressing ingredients in a small bowl and pour over the barley salad. Toss gently. Sprinkle the extra mint and parsley leaves as well as pomegranate seeds on the salad.

Watermelon, Kalamata olive and feta summer salad

I remember watching my uncle George standing by the kitchen sink, eating fresh watermelon with feta. I would stare at him, shocked at the odd combination. He would say how refreshing and delicious it was and suggest I try it. Of course I wouldn't at the time, but I have since, and have to agree that it is truly delicious. The unusual pairing features in this summer salad – the barley rusk is optional, but I just love the extra texture it brings.

4 large barley rusks
1 kg watermelon, seeded and
   cut into 1 cm cubes
200 g Greek feta, cut into
   5 mm cubes
1 small red onion, finely
   chopped
3 tablespoons finely chopped
   flat-leaf parsley
3 tablespoons finely chopped
   mint
3 tablespoons Kalamata
   olives, pitted, rinsed and
   roughly chopped

Dressing
4–5 tablespoons extra virgin
   olive oil
1 teaspoon ground cumin
1 clove garlic, crushed
1 tablespoon red wine vinegar
sea salt and cracked pepper
1 tablespoon lemon juice
grated zest of ½ lemon

Serves 4

Place a barley rusk in the centre of each plate, then pile a quarter of the watermelon on top and sprinkle with a quarter each of the feta and onion. Add the parsley and mint, followed by the olives. Alternatively, place the rusks on a serving dish. Combine the remaining salad ingredients in a bowl and pile them on top of the rusks.

Combine the dressing ingredients in a small bowl and pour over the salad. Set aside for 5 minutes before serving, so that the rusks soak up some of the juices.

My Kalamata heritage

Although I never had an opportunity to meet my grandmother on my mother's side, and I was very young when my mother died, I feel very connected to both women from the stories that my beloved aunt Stavroula has shared with me.

My grandmother, Amalia Davos, was born and lived in the municipality of Arcadia in a town called Dirahia, in Peloponnesus. She was the youngest of nine children: seven daughters and two sons. Her brothers Dimitri and Athanasi both became priests. Many members of my grandmother's family have taken on religious duties and this may account for our family's strong Greek Orthodox faith and the powerful influence it has had on our cooking.

When my grandmother Amalia married she moved to Kalamata. As was the tradition, she was gifted with a dowry, prepared by her mother and other family members. It consisted of bed linen, towels and other handmade treasures. Her father also gave her a furnished house as a wedding gift. The dowry tradition dates back to classical times and represented the woman's inheritance, given by her father or family, on the occasion of her marriage. It formed a kind of fund to provide her with security in her future life with her husband. A dowry would consist of not just belongings and land but also animals such as goats, and would be agreed upon between the father of the bride and the bridegroom either verbally or in writing before the marriage.

My grandmother had three children: my aunt Stavroula, uncle Panagioti and my mother, Ioanna. My grandmother's primary responsibility was the running of the household. My grandfather, Christo Davos, had a small shop where he sold cotton, ribbon, needles, paints and other little things.

Amalia was an extremely resourceful woman. She enjoyed making things and there was nothing that she could not do. The family relied on the land around them for their food and they made everything they needed, including the furniture, towels and sheets. My grandmother would spin the wool to make the decorative rugs and my mother and aunt would complete the embroidery. All household items would be embroidered to make them look special. We have used some of this delicate handiwork to decorate the pages of this book.

The war years

My aunt recalls that her early childhood in Kalamata was a happy time for her and her family. During Lent she would assist her mother to prepare the Easter sweet bread called *kouloures* (in other parts of Greece it is known as *tsoureki* – see recipe on page 140). The dough was moulded into the shape of a flower wreath. My aunt would then create small flower designs to decorate the wreath before finally preparing red-painted eggs and carefully arranging these on the wreath. The *kouloures* would then be baked slowly in the oven before being hung on the wall for 40 days, finally being consumed on Easter day. The aroma from the bread would leave the whole house smelling sweet for days.

My aunt also recalls the times she would help her mother to prepare a dish called *stifado*. This would be prepared on days before Christmas fasting commenced. My aunt enjoyed making this dish and it is now one of her favourites. She makes it often as a tribute to my grandmother and as a way of remembering her. I have included a recipe for octopus *stifado* on page 129 and rabbit *stifado* on page 175 of this book.

When the Second World War came to Greece in 1941 there was unrest, hunger and hardship. The churches were not permitted to hold services. Our family became very poor and my grandfather was ordered to close his shop. My aunt was seven, her brother was two years old and my mother was a baby of nine months.

My grandfather Christo, who was then 35 years old, came home one day with tears in his eyes and announced that he had been conscripted.

The next day the family went to the train station to see him off. My aunt recalls the many tears shed that day. They were all distraught, not knowing whether they would see him again.

When the Germans and Italians came to Kalamata, everyone in the village was extremely frightened and anxious. At the Independence Day memorial in the centre of town the Germans placed two sacks on the ground. One contained potatoes and the other lentils. On the potato sack they wrote the word 'Greece' and on the lentil sack they wrote 'Germany'. The sacks represented the numbers of Greeks and Germans by population. They then announced that if anyone should kill a German then one lentil would go but 50 Greeks would then be killed to avenge the crime. It was a stern warning of what would happen if anybody upset the Germans or their allies, the Italians.

It was no longer possible to make rich dishes such as *stifado* during the war as all of the family's produce and many of their personal belongings were requisitioned by the Germans. The family struggled to survive and many friends and neighbours passed away from hunger. As a young child my aunt witnessed several deaths, including that of her grandfather, whom she initially thought had simply been taking a long nap.

Food, particularly meat, was in short supply and the citizens of Kalamata were forced to survive on a predominantly vegetarian diet. Olive oil, rice and bread were also non-existent. My aunt recalls that a close neighbour, to save his family from starvation, was forced to sell his home for a goat, a sack of flour and a tin of olive oil.

Despite these obstacles my grandmother still managed to invent new recipes with what little she had. They had dried figs (for which Kalamata is renowned), wild greens hidden high up in the mountains, walnuts, oranges, cauliflower and plenty of snails. The snails seemed to have appeared miraculously, as if God had opened the heavens and showered the snails over Kalamata to nourish the starving Greeks, my aunt would say.

Given the abundance of snails, snail-based dishes often featured on the menu and wild greens with snails became a regular dish in the Davos household. Today my aunt cannot bear to cook or eat snails. They are a painful reminder to her of the *katohi* – the years of war and foreign occupation.

During the war the Italians occupied the school close to my family's home. It was converted into an army base. Although she did not know how to speak Italian, my aunt did learn the words, '*Signore, un poco pane?*' meaning, 'Sir, a little bread?' She would often visit the soldiers and watch them consume their plentiful supplies of food – food that had been taken from the people of Kalamata. Although she was frightened of them, she was famished and hoped that they would pity her and offer her some scraps of food to take home to her family. Sometimes they would give her leftover bread or perhaps some spaghetti in a pot. She would then quickly run home and share the food with her family, before returning to the soldiers with the sparkling clean pot.

It was not unusual for raids on the homes of Greek civilians to occur during the German occupation. On one occasion the Germans appeared unannounced and forced their way into my grandmother's home. They were searching for guns, refugees who may be hiding and anything of value they could take. In a corner of the house they spotted a crate made out of English planks and became suspicious. The Germans recognised the wood as English and wrongfully assumed it contained weapons. In fact, my grandmother used the crate to store dried figs and walnuts. The soldiers hit the crate with their guns and broke it open. The figs and walnuts rolled across the floor. One of the soldiers grabbed a handful of dried figs and greedily began to eat them. The other soldier immediately knocked them out of his hands. Perhaps he recognised just how hungry the family had become. Curiously, they then nailed the crate back together and quickly left.

My grandmother's family endured many difficulties during the war. However, despite all the trials, they always remained a close, harmonious, generous and loving family.

Growing up hearing these stories has not only given me a deeper appreciation for food but has also reinforced how privileged I am to live in Australia – a place where there is peace, an abundance of meat, seafood, fresh fruit and vegetables. Not only am I able to obtain the produce that Australia is renowned for, but also the items I cherish from Greece, such as good-quality olive oil, olives, figs and sea urchins.

After the war

My grandfather Christo survived the war and returned to a very different Kalamata to the town he had left. My grandmother Amalia had to find work to support the family. She had not worked before, but as they had lost everything she had no choice.

She began work in a fig factory in Kalamata. The economy was beginning to recover and besides olives and olive oil, figs were the next biggest export. My grandmother's job was to carefully arrange the figs in wooden boxes. Another lady would then wrap and seal the box tightly. Each box would fit twelve figs perfectly.

It was imperative that the three children each learn a trade. Panagioti studied to become an electrician and my mother and Stavroula learnt to sew. My aunt finished school at fifth grade and began working at fourteen and a half to support the family and to help rebuild what they had lost during the war.

Panagioti found work on a ship as an electrician. On one voyage he came to Australia and instantly fell in love with the country. He could see that it was full of opportunity, and so resolved that he would live there and work hard to make a better life for himself and his family. While on the ship he met Mr Gouma, the then vice-consul of the Greek embassy in Australia. They formed a very close friendship and Mr Gouma was able to assist my uncle to acquire his Australian citizenship.

The move to Australia

My grandmother, grandfather and mother came to Australia in 1959 to join Panagioti. My aunt Stavroula remained behind. By that stage

Stavroula had married and her husband, George Kargas, was reluctant to emigrate. He had established a menswear shop in Kalamata and was happy there. However, my aunt missed her brother Panagioti and her parents too much, so reluctantly my uncle decided to sell his shop and come to Australia too. They were both worried and apprehensive about the move; they did not know what Australia would be like and neither of them spoke a word of English.

They packed their entire lives into a few suitcases and a chest and, with their two young sons, Chris and Manny, boarded the vessel the *Patris*. In the chest my aunt packed 100 tins of *Vlahas* milk – she was worried that Australia would not have any milk with which to feed her children. She also packed other food items, including 20 packets of *myzithra* cheese, 100 tins of artichokes and 100 tins of okra. As well as these 'essentials' they brought their two sewing machines.

For three months after their arrival in Sydney, my uncle ordered my aunt not to unpack; he wanted to return to Greece. My aunt, however, did not want to leave. She adapted quickly and wanted to remain with the family members of hers who had settled in Sydney. Eventually, my uncle George adapted to Australia and the family began to settle in. They first lived in Palmer Street, Darlinghurst, before moving to Coogee.

My grandmother Amalia, mother Ioanna
and grandfather Christo in their first home
in Darlinghurst shortly after emigrating

My mother Ioanna, My aunt Stavroula
and uncle Panagioti in Kalamata

Aunt Stavroula, uncle George and cousins
Chris and Manny in the passport photo →
before emigrating to Australia

My grandmother Amalia's brother, Dimitrios Tzouvelis, was a priest
in Kalamata. The photo of the Tzouvelis family includes my
aunt Stavroula (far left) and mother Ioanna (second from right).

Santorini salad

This salad makes use of all the fabulous produce Santorini is famous for: capers, caper leaves, volcanic cucumbers and tomatoes, anchovies and the local hard cheese. You can find caper leaves at any good Greek delicatessen, but if you don't have one nearby, just use extra capers. I use either *kefalotiri* or *kefalograviera* cheese for this salad, depending on what I have in the fridge. *Kefalotiri* is a hard yellow cheese made of goat or sheep's milk. *Kefalograviera* is made of sheep and cow's milk and has a mild slightly salty flavour.

400 g small tomatoes
1 Lebanese cucumber
½ cup capers, rinsed and
   drained
3 tablespoons caper leaves,
   drained
8 anchovy fillets
50 g *kefalotiri* or *kefalograviera*
   cheese, shaved
½ teaspoon dried wild
   oregano
sea salt
2–3 tablespoons extra virgin
   olive oil

Serves 4

Wash the tomatoes, cut them in half and arrange on a serving plate. Thickly slice the cucumber into rounds and add to the plate with the capers and caper leaves. Garnish with the anchovy fillets and shaved cheese.

Sprinkle with the oregano and a very small amount of sea salt – the anchovies are quite salty so you don't need a lot. Drizzle the olive oil over the top and serve.

Salad from Crete

This refreshing salad is one of my favourites, and combines two ingredients that Crete is famous for: barley rusks and extra virgin olive oil. The people of Crete live close to nature and respect it in a way that I have never witnessed elsewhere. Their pure organic diet – high in extra virgin olive oil, fruits and vegetables – must be one of the main reasons for their low rate of heart disease and long life expectancy. It's very inspiring.

In Crete they usually use a local cheese, *anthotiro*, for this salad. This can be difficult to find outside Greece, so I have improvised and come up with my own version: fresh ricotta infused in rosewater. It bears no resemblance to the slightly salty *anthotiro*, but somehow it works anyway.

2 tablespoons fresh ricotta
½ cup rosewater
1 large barley rusk
5 large ripe tomatoes
sea salt
½ cup extra virgin olive oil
  (preferably from Crete)
1 teaspoon dried wild oregano
½ cup chopped mint

Serves 2

Mould the ricotta into a ball shape, wrap in a piece of cheese cloth and tie it up so the ricotta keeps its shape. Place in a small bowl and pour the rosewater over it, then leave to infuse in the fridge for at least 4 hours.

Place the barley rusk on a serving plate and set aside.

Cut the tomatoes in half and remove the stem. Grate the meat side of the tomato using a coarse vegetable grater over a bowl so that you are left with the pulp. Discard the skin.

Combine the grated tomato, salt, olive oil, oregano and all but ½ teaspoon of the mint in a bowl. Pour this over the rusks and leave for about 5 minutes so that the rusk soaks up the juices.

Remove the ricotta from the cheese cloth and place on top of the tomato mixture. Garnish with the remaining mint and serve.

Cyclades potato salad

The ingredients in this salad embody the Cyclades islands, which I adore.

1–1.5 kg potatoes, washed
sea salt and cracked pepper
1 Lebanese cucumber, seeded
 and chopped
½ cup capers, rinsed and
 drained
6 spring onions, finely
 chopped
3 tablespoons finely
 chopped dill
3 tablespoons chopped
 flat-leaf parsley
¼ cup extra virgin olive oil
½ teaspoon dried wild oregano
3 tablespoons lemon juice
1 tablespoon Greek-style
 yoghurt
3 tablespoons caper leaves,
 drained
8 anchovy fillets

Serves 4–6

Place the potatoes in a saucepan, add cold water and salt and bring to the boil. Cook for 15–20 minutes until the potatoes are tender but not falling apart, then drain and leave to cool for 5 minutes. Remove the skin, cut into pieces and place in a bowl.

Add the cucumber, capers, spring onion, dill and parsley and mix gently.

In a small bowl combine the olive oil, oregano, salt, pepper, lemon juice and yoghurt. Pour over the potato salad and gently toss.

Arrange the caper leaves and anchovy fillets on top, and serve warm or chilled.

Radish and currant salad >

I love the peppery taste of radishes, and when combined with sweet currants, the two balance out perfectly. Serve with any seafood or meat dish.

1 bunch radishes
3 tablespoons currants

Dressing
1 tablespoon chopped mint
1–2 tablespoons lemon juice
2 tablespoons olive oil
2 tablespoons Greek-style
 yoghurt
1 teaspoon honey
½ teaspoon ground cumin
pinch of sea salt

Serves 4

Wash the radishes well, then pat dry and thinly slice (you need about 2 cups). I use a mandoline or vegetable slicer to do this – it's much quicker than using a knife, and ensures the slices are the same thickness. Place them in a bowl with the currants.

Mix together the dressing ingredients, toss through the radishes and currants and serve.

< Haloumi, basil and tomato salad

I usually make this simple salad for lunch and have it with some crusty bread. The combination of *haloumi*, basil and tomato also works beautifully in an omelette. You can use any tomatoes you like – I often use a mixture of grape, roma and other small varieties to give a good splash of colour.

200 g small roma or grape
   tomatoes, or a mixture
sea salt and cracked pepper
250 g *haloumi*, cut into 5 even
   slices (of about 5 mm each)
1 tablespoon Greek ouzo
1 tablespoon lemon juice
¼ cup chopped basil
½ teaspoon dried wild
   oregano
3 tablespoons extra virgin
   olive oil

Serves 2

Wash the tomatoes and cut them in half. Arrange on a round serving platter, leaving a space in the middle for the *haloumi*. Season the tomatoes with a little salt.

Heat a lightly oiled chargrill pan. When hot, cook the *haloumi* on both sides until the pieces are slightly brown. Add the ouzo and let the alcohol cook off. Remove from the heat and drizzle with the lemon juice.

Place the *haloumi* in the middle of the platter and season with pepper. Sprinkle the basil over the tomatoes and *haloumi*.

In a bowl, mix together the oregano, olive oil and a little sea salt. Drizzle over the salad and serve while the *haloumi* is still warm.

Walnut, fig, kasseri and pastourma salad

I love the combination of fig, *kasseri* and *pastourma*, served simply as here, or wrapped in filo as a *meze*. *Kasseri* works particularly well with bread and fresh fruit, while *pastourma* has a fabulous texture and colour, and a peppery flavour that complements anything sweet or sour. I sometimes add red seedless grapes to this salad. If you can't find *kasseri*, use *kefalotiri* or *kefalograviera* as a substitute.

8 slices *pastourma*
3 tablespoons walnuts
100 g wild rocket
1 small red onion,
   thinly sliced
4 fresh figs, cut into quarters
50 g *kasseri*, shaved
3 tablespoons extra virgin
   olive oil
1 tablespoon lemon juice
sea salt

Serves 4

Preheat the oven to 150°C. Place the *pastourma* in a baking dish and bake for 5–10 minutes until it darkens in colour and becomes a bit crunchy. Set aside to cool.

Reduce the oven temperature to 130°C. Spread out the walnuts on a baking tray and toast until lightly golden. Set aside to cool.

Arrange the rocket on a serving platter and scatter the onion, walnuts and figs over the top. Place the *pastourma* in the middle and top with the *kasseri*.

In a small bowl, mix together the olive oil, lemon juice and a little sea salt. Drizzle over the salad and serve.

Zesty pomegranate and pastourma salad

In Greece it is not unusual to see a pomegranate tree in almost every yard. They bear beautiful red fruit, full of juicy red seeds. Like the fig, the pomegranate is sacred in Greece, symbolising fertility, love and death. At some weddings a pomegranate is broken on the ground as a symbol of abundance, fertility and good luck. And when the Greeks commemorate their dead they make *kolliva*, which is decorated with pomegranate seeds (see page 203).

In this salad, the sweetness of the pomegranate and the pepperiness of the *pastourma* go perfectly with the crunchy salad vegetables.

5 slices *pastourma*
200–300 g mesclun salad
  greens
1 carrot, peeled
1 cucumber, peeled
seeds of 1 pomegranate
1–2 cloves garlic, crushed
1 teaspoon ground cumin
1 teaspoon grated lemon zest
2 tablespoons lemon juice
1 tablespoon red wine vinegar
3 tablespoons extra virgin
  olive oil
sea salt
1 red pear, grated

Serves 4

Preheat the oven to 150°C. Place the *pastourma* in a baking dish and bake for 5–10 minutes until it darkens in colour and becomes a bit crunchy. Cool to room temperature.

Place the salad greens in a large mixing bowl. Using a mandolin or vegetable slicer, thinly slice the carrot and cucumber and add to the greens.

Process half the pomegranate seeds in a blender, then strain the juice into a large glass. Add the garlic, cumin, lemon zest and juice, vinegar, olive oil and salt and mix well. Pour over the salad.

Add the grated pear to the bowl and toss well. Transfer into a serving bowl and add the *pastourma* (when serving individual portions, break the *pastourma* into pieces).
Sprinkle the remaining pomegranate seeds on top and serve.

Me with my grandmother, Katina Benardis,
who passed away in March 2009

My passport photo at the age of five

A picture of me, my cousin John, and
sister Katina, taken in Psara, Greece,
when I was three, in 1971

A view of the little beach that I used
to play on in Psara. The church that is
visible is the church of Aghios Nickolaos,
which my family still helps maintain.

Special delivery to Psara

When I was three and a half years old my younger sister and I went to live on the island of Psara, Greece. My mother was very ill with cancer and my father sent us to live there with his mother, Katina. We didn't know it at the time but our mother succumbed to cancer shortly after we left.

I can still vividly recall the frightening and unfamiliar flight to Athens. My sister and I, along with another baby in a bassinette, sat at the back of the plane with the airhostess who had been appointed to take care of us. The baby cried for most of the flight, as did my sister in sympathy. When we eventually landed in Athens my sister did not want to be separated from the baby. She cried and screamed loudly that it was her baby doll. If I board a plane today and happen to see children travelling unaccompanied, my mind travels back to that first flight to Greece with my sister, and even though it was such a traumatic time, I can't help but smile at the memory now.

Psara is a small, remote, mountainous island to the northeast of Athens. Surrounded by tempestuous seas and with an enormous lighthouse (*faros*) on one side of the island to help prevent shipwrecks, it has an abandoned look and feel about it.

My sister and I were in a state of culture shock for some time after we arrived. We knew a few words of Greek because our parents had spoken the language to us, but we were by no means fluent. I was very confused and sad about leaving Australia. I could not understand why I had to leave and why my mother and father had not come with me. I tried to find ways to deal with the emptiness and loneliness I felt. I would imagine having parties with my mother and father. When my grandmother gave me some goat's milk to drink I would request an extra glass. The extra milk was to share with my parents, I would tell her.

My grandmother was very strict and regimented with us two girls. It wasn't an easy life for her – my grandfather had gone off to war and left her with four sons to raise. And then when she should have been taking it easy, she was sent a special delivery of two toddlers to look after. But it was through my grandmother, on this strange island that became my home, that I developed my passion for food.

I loved to go on walking expeditions around the island. One day, while on one of my regular walks, I stumbled across a small enclosed, deserted area, with just a few weeds growing. I decided that it was now going to be mine and that I would create my own magical fruit and vegetable garden. I decided not to tell anybody about it, especially not my grandmother. To create my garden I took some of the herbs and vegetables my grandmother grew and planted them there. I grew all sorts of things: small tomatoes, thyme, oregano, wild greens, zucchinis, chamomile leaves and native flowers. It was an extremely colourful and happy garden and it became my favourite place on the island – somewhere I could escape to, to dream and be free. I derived great joy from watching my plants grow. I also loved to sit in my little garden perched high above the sea, to watch the fishermen bring in their catch and tenderise the octopus by bashing it on the rocks.

Life on the island was busy but, in many respects, simple. We had no electricity or flushing toilets. Our major form of transport was the donkey. Most of our food was grown in our garden and our cooking was performed outdoors in the fresh breezy sea air. My grandmother would bake our bread, and make cheese and yoghurt with our goat's milk. It was not any easy life but it was a happy one. I had my chores each morning, which included feeding the chickens and collecting the eggs, milking the goat, and picking the herbs and vegetables.

Our diet was predominantly made up of seafood and vegetables because this was what surrounded us. Meat dishes were rare and a luxury, reserved for special occasions. It was also very important for us to preserve some of the produce for the winter months so that we would always have plenty of food to eat. In the summertime I would help my grandmother put tomatoes and the various teas (like chamomile) on the roof to dry. We would then store these in large pottery jars ready for the winter months.

My grandmother and the other women on the island were obsessed with cooking food using fresh, organic produce. We had sea urchin, bread, cheese, vegetables and seafood on the table every night. We would occasionally have goat and rabbit, but I was not happy about eating rabbit. I had rabbits that visited my garden and I was afraid that I might be eating one I had formed a friendship with.

My grandmother never found out about my garden and I never told her about it for fear that it might be taken from me. I would harvest some of the produce from my garden and take it to my grandmother, telling her it was from ours. There were times when she could not understand how the zucchinis had grown so big given that the day before they had been half the size. I would tell her that I had sung the songs she had taught me and I had given them a kiss to let them know that I loved them. They had responded by growing quicker. She'd be puzzled and surprised but she would say no more.

I cherished the times I cooked with my grandmother. I preferred this to playing with the other kids on the island. Sometimes our neighbours would come and we would all cook together, singing and dancing as we worked. There would always be a prayer in between to bless the food and thank God for helping it grow and multiply. The ingredients were always handled with care and with respect. To this day I follow these principles when cooking, as I believe it makes the food tastier and more flavoursome.

The main entertainment on Psara was the many feasts and festivals. Practically all of the 420 inhabitants of the island would come together to celebrate birthdays and name days. Each family would cook a dish and we would all share and eat the food. We would also sing and dance to traditional folk music. Food was an integral and vital component of our celebrations. It was our way of showing our love for the person or saint we were honouring and the people around us.

While living on Psara, a monumental event happened to me. I had a terrible fall and broke my arm. I had to go to Chios with my grandmother to have my arm set in plaster, because this could not be done on the island of Psara. It was in Chios that I first encountered capers, caper leaves, rose petal sweets and the mastic tree. I had never smelt anything so sweet and beautiful as mastic gum (*masticha*). My grandmother and I brought back all of these ingredients from Chios, which we used to make many delicious dishes. I still enjoy using these ingredients in my cooking; they remind me of the day in Chios when I discovered them.

A number of years later, when I was about nine, my sister and I returned to Australia to live with our father, who had called for our return, and our new stepmother. I vividly recall it being one of the saddest days of my life. Despite my initial resistance to moving to Psara, I had formed a connection with and love for the people, the food, the culture and the island itself. For the first time in my life I felt that I belonged. When I came back to Australia, I missed my garden, the sea, the mountains, watching the fishermen bring in the seafood, and the simple life. My experiences in Psara, I believe, have been the key reasons for my obsession with cooking organic, fresh, vibrant dishes. I have many happy memories of Psara and I still miss the island. I love to cook the dishes we ate so often. This connects me to that part of the world, where a piece of my heart and soul remains.

ό Χαβρίου Κ...

ταῖς γυναιξὶ λαμ...

Μένανδρος δ' ἐν 'Οργῇ...

καίτοι νέος ποτ' ἐγενόμην κα...

ἀλλ' οὐκ ἐλούμην πεντάκις τῆς...

τότ', ἀλλὰ νῦν· οὐδὲ χλανίδ' εἶχον...

29 PAA 587475, Chabrias (PA 15086) was an impo...
was general who died in combat in 357/6 BCE, hence th...
public hono[u]rs to commemor[ate] his monument. Phaedrias (PA 1...
otherwise unknown.

Meze

The aim of serving *meze* is to stimulate the appetite, not to satisfy it. The word *meze* means 'middle', as in middle of the day, or between meals, so it follows that it is usually eaten at lunchtime or before dinner. It is a slow grazing session with friends and family and is accompanied by wine or a spirit such as *ouzo* or *tsipouro*.

A *meze* plate is perfect for when you are entertaining and need some nibbles with drinks or as a starter at the dinner table, and the eye-catching array of Greek delicacies is sure to keep the conversation flowing.

My meze plate

These recipes will allow you to create the perfect meze *plate for any occasion. Begin by making the* taramosalata, tzatziki, *herbed yoghurt dip and* tirokafteri, *as these require some time to chill in the fridge before serving. An hour or so before serving, prepare the roast baby tomatoes, the olives and the* pastourma. *Just before your guests arrive, prepare the sea urchin,* avgotaracho *and figs. Finish off the platter with some pickled vegetables from your pantry. Place some small barley rusks on another platter and serve them with the* mezedes. *Serves 6*

Taramosalata

To make any *taramosalata* a success you must start with good-quality stale bread, such as Vienna or sourdough. You can use spelt bread if you have a wheat intolerance. Of equal importance is the quality of the *tarama* (sea-mullet roe). I use the tinned variety, which you can get at any good delicatessen – it gives the *taramosalata* a lovely creamy colour and texture.

1 loaf stale Vienna or
    sourdough bread, crusts
    removed
100 g *tarama*
2 spring onions, chopped
1 clove garlic, chopped
¾ cup lemon juice
½ cup extra virgin olive oil

Makes about 1½ cups

Soak the bread in a bowl of water until softened. Remove and squeeze out any excess water.

Place the bread in a blender and process until it has formed crumbs. Add the *tarama*, spring onion and garlic and blend for a few seconds.

Gradually add the lemon juice and then the olive oil and blend until the mixture forms a smooth paste. You may need to add a little more olive oil to achieve your desired consistency.

Cover and refrigerate for a few hours, then serve with crusty country-style bread or small barley rusks.

Tzatziki

Tzatziki can be eaten as a *meze*, dip or as an accompaniment for seafood, *souvlaki*, *gyros* and so on. Make it the night before if you can to give the flavours time to develop, but add the herb garnish just before serving.

sea salt
1 Lebanese cucumber, peeled, seeded and finely chopped
500 g Greek-style yoghurt
2–3 cloves garlic, crushed
2 tablespoons olive oil
2 tablespoons chopped mint, dill or basil

Makes 2 cups

Sprinkle some sea salt over the chopped cucumber and allow to stand for about 10 minutes.

Take small amounts of cucumber in your hands and squeeze out any liquid. Place the squeezed cucumber in a bowl. Add the yoghurt, garlic and olive oil and mix gently.

Refrigerate for at least 2 hours, then garnish with the chopped herbs and serve.

Herbed yoghurt dip

This dip contains basil, one of my favourite herbs. The Greek word for basil is *vasillikos*, which means 'royal' – very fitting as basil is the crowning herb in Greek cuisine. It is also used in the Greek Orthodox Church to bless its patrons and to bless people's homes. As with all ingredients, basil must be handled delicately and respectfully.

This dip is divine served simply with crusty bread. I also enjoy dipping my *dolmades* in it (see recipe on page 61).

2 spring onions, chopped
2–3 cloves garlic, sliced
1 cup roughly chopped flat-leaf parsley
1 cup roughly chopped dill
3 tablespoons roughly chopped mint
½ cup roughly chopped basil
1–2 tablespoons lemon juice
2–3 tablespoons olive oil
500 g Greek-style yoghurt

Makes 2 cups

Place the spring onion, garlic and herbs in a blender and process for about 1 minute or until finely chopped. Add the lemon juice and olive oil and blend for a further 30 seconds or until smooth.

Spoon the yoghurt into a bowl, add the mixture from the blender and fold through gently until well combined. Refrigerate for at least 2 hours before serving.

Clockwise from left:
Pickled vegetables, roast baby
tomatoes, *pastourma*, barley rusks,
tzatziki, *taramosalata*, herbed
yoghurt dip, rosemary and garlic
Kalamata olives, and sea urchin

Tirokafteri

'*Tiro*' is derived from the Greek word *tiri* (cheese) and *kafteri* means hot, so essentially *tirokafteri* means a hot cheese. Traditionally it is made with feta and hot peppers or chillies, but my version has a few extras. It is a perfect accompaniment to *ouzo*.

250 g Greek feta, cubed
1 tablespoon Greek-style
  yoghurt
1 tablespoon extra virgin
  olive oil
1 clove garlic, crushed
½ teaspoon dried wild
  oregano
1–2 small fresh chillies,
  seeded and finely chopped
handful of basil leaves
2 spring onions, chopped
cracked pepper

Makes 1– 1½ cups

Combine all the ingredients in a blender and mix really well. Refrigerate for at least a couple of hours before serving.

Roast baby tomatoes

A Greek dinner table would not be complete without a tomato-based dish. This is a quick and easy way to enjoy good-quality tomatoes.

8 small vine-ripened
  tomatoes, left whole
1 tablespoon red wine vinegar
2 tablespoons extra virgin
  olive oil
sea salt and cracked pepper

Makes 8

Preheat the oven to 200°C.

Place the tomatoes in a baking dish and drizzle with the red wine vinegar and olive oil. Season with salt and pepper, and roast for 5–10 minutes, until they just begin to soften. Set aside to cool.

Pickled vegetables

The Greek word for pickled vegetables is *trousi*. They are generally made with salt, vinegar and a couple of spices, but I have added a few more ingredients – such as *masticha* (mastic chewing gum) – to spice up the vegetables and make them uniquely Greek.

1 small piece of *masticha*
¾ cup castor sugar
½ white cabbage, washed
5 carrots, peeled
sea salt
1 teaspoon fennel seeds
1 teaspoon ground allspice
6 whole black peppercorns
1 cinnamon stick
4 whole cloves
1 litre red wine vinegar

Fills a 2-litre jar

Sterilise a 2-litre glass jar with boiling water, and have two small pieces of white cotton cloth or cheese cloth to hand.

Place the *masticha* in a mortar and pestle with 1 teaspoon of the castor sugar and grind until it forms a powder. Tip the mixture onto one of the pieces of cloth and tie tightly with kitchen string.

Cut the cabbage in half, remove the core and cut into 2 cm thick slices. Thinly slice the carrots with a vegetable slicer.

Bring a large saucepan of salted water to the boil, add the cabbage and simmer for 1 minute until slightly softened. Remove the cabbage and drain well in a colander. Boil the carrots for 1 minute until slightly softened, then drain. Place the carrots and cabbage in the sterilised jar.

Combine the salt, fennel seeds, allspice, peppercorns, cinnamon stick and cloves in a saucepan and heat for a little while, stirring to release the aromas.

Add the vinegar and the *masticha* cloth bundle and bring gently to the boil. Simmer for a couple of minutes, then remove from the heat and pour into the jar, right to the top. Cool to room temperature.

Place the cloth over the top of the jar, followed by the lid and seal the jar. Store in a dark place for at least 1–2 months before eating – the longer you leave them the better the flavour will be. Finely slice the vegetables before serving.

Rosemary and garlic Kalamata olives

The Kalamata olive is the quintessential Greek olive. They are usually sold in brine and can be extremely salty, which is why I often rinse them. Here, the garlic and rosemary are the perfect foil for the smooth, earthy flavour of the olives.

20 Kalamata olives
1 tablespoon extra virgin
    olive oil
1 clove garlic, crushed
1 teaspoon chopped rosemary

Makes 20

Rinse the olives and drain well. Gently pat them dry with kitchen paper.

Heat the olive oil in a skillet or frying pan over low heat, add the garlic and cook until golden brown. Add the olives and rosemary and toss through for a couple of minutes. Transfer to a bowl and leave to cool.

Avgotaracho >

Avgotaracho is the orange-coloured roe of mullet, which has been pressed, smoked and encased in beeswax. It has a caramelised salt-fish flavour and is a great way to tease one's appetite before the main meal.

1 piece *avgotaracho*
1 lemon, cut into wedges

Serves 4–6

Remove the thin layer of wax from the *avgotaracho* and thinly slice or shred it. Serve with lemon wedges.

Pastourma >

Pastourma is a pungent cured beef that has usually been rubbed with spices and herbs such as fenugreek. It is produced in many regions in Greece, particularly those close to Turkey.

8 slices *pastourma*

Makes 8

Preheat the oven to 180°C.

Place the *pastourma* slices in a baking dish and bake for 5–10 minutes until it darkens in colour and becomes a bit crunchy. Set aside to cool.

Sea urchin

I prefer to buy whole fresh sea urchins. I always put them in the freezer for an hour or so to put them to sleep before I start cooking.

6 fresh sea urchins
sea salt
1 lemon, cut into wedges

Makes 6

Open the sea urchins and remove the orange roe with a paring knife. Discard the rest.

Place the sea urchin fillets on a corner of the serving platter. Sprinkle with sea salt and serve with the lemon wedges.

Figs with anchovy fillets >

In ancient Greece dried figs were eaten as an appetiser or served with wine. I created this dish using fresh figs to pay tribute to this long-standing tradition.

4 fresh figs, cut in half
16 anchovy fillets
1 spring onion, thinly sliced
1 tablespoon chopped
   flat-leaf parsley
cracked pepper
extra virgin olive oil,
   for drizzling

Makes 8

Arrange the fig halves on a *meze* platter and place two anchovy fillets on each half. Sprinkle with spring onion and parsley, season with pepper and drizzle a little olive oil over the top.

Stavroula's passion for food

My aunt Stavroula Kargas is the most important influence in my life.
Not only has she been a mother figure to me, she is also one of the most
inspirational people I have met. I have always found her passion for
food intoxicating. She has enriched me with everything I needed to
know about good-quality traditional Greek cuisine. She has also passed
on to me all of my grandmother Amalia's recipes and traditions.

My sister and I returned from Psara to Sydney to live for a brief time
with our father and stepmother. Then when I was about 12 years old
the two of us were adopted by my aunt Stavroula and her family.
I remember my aunt would always be in the kitchen cooking; it was
the most utilised room in the house. She was extremely fussy and
meticulous in the kitchen, carefully peeling each mushroom and
cleaning each individual whitebait before deep-frying it. She always
used the best and freshest ingredients. Nothing else was good enough
for her dishes. If she went to a local greengrocer and things weren't
up to her high standard, she would demand that we all pile back into
the car and drive somewhere else to buy our provisions.

My aunt is very reserved when it comes to expressing her feelings. Her
affection is expressed through the dishes she cooks. She loves cooking
for people and everyone who comes to her table is always well fed.
People visiting our place would comment that they had not eaten all
day to prepare themselves for the upcoming feast and that they would
probably not eat for a few days afterwards! The dishes she still creates
are always magical and representative of how she feels about those with
whom she shares the food. I always feel loved and special around her.

I thank her for enriching my life with her food philosophies and recipes,
and I am privileged to be able to share some of them with you in the
pages of this book.

Ouzo-spiked oysters >

This recipe adopts the ancient Greek principle of finding harmony between sweet, salty and sour flavours. I have used fish sauce, or *garos* as it was called in ancient Greece, to enhance the salty element.

12 freshly shucked oysters
1 tablespoon finely chopped
   dill
1 tablespoon finely chopped
   spring onion

Dressing
3 tablespoons *ouzo*
4 tablespoons lemon juice
2 tablespoons fish sauce

Makes 12

Combine all the dressing ingredients, then taste to ensure it is balanced. Adjust the quantities if necessary to suit your palate.

Arrange the oysters on a plate and drizzle about 1 teaspoon of the dressing over each oyster. Garnish with a little dill and spring onion.

Mastic-infused mayonnaise

This is a perfect accompaniment to seafood, and goes beautifully with deep-fried cumin calamari (see page 120). If the mayonnaise becomes too thick, beat in a little water until you reach the desired consistency.

350 ml extra virgin olive oil
1 large crystal *masticha*
2 egg yolks, at room
   temperature
pinch of sea salt
pinch of white pepper

Makes about 1½ cups

Pour enough olive oil into a non-stick frying pan to cover the base and set over medium heat. When the oil has heated, add the *masticha* and stir with a metal spoon until it dissolves. Remove from the heat immediately and pour into a 350 ml glass jar. Add the remaining olive oil and fill the jar to the top. Cool to room temperature.

Using a hand whisk or a blender, whisk together the egg yolks and salt. Whisking constantly, gradually add the mastic-infused olive oil in a thin, steady stream until the mayonnaise is thick and velvety. Add the pepper, and season with additional salt and pepper if you like.

Pour the mayonnaise into a small bowl, cover and refrigerate before serving.

Chestnut skordalia

Skordalia is a Greek garlic dip. It makes a great accompaniment to seafood and wild greens, and I particularly love it with deep-fried artichoke or served simply with crusty bread. I often make it out of mashed potato or bread, with a handful of walnuts or almonds thrown in (see recipe below), but this chestnut version is one of my favourite recipes.

2 cups fresh chestnuts
4 cloves garlic, peeled
sea salt and cracked pepper
½ cup olive oil
extra virgin olive oil

Makes about 1½ cups

Lay each chestnut on its side and cut halfway around the outer shell. Place the chestnuts in a saucepan of cold water and bring to the boil. Cover and simmer for 15–20 minutes or until the shell opens and the flesh is soft. Remove the shell and peel off the brown outer layer of skin to reveal the white flesh.

Place the peeled chestnuts in a blender while they are still hot and process to a smooth paste. Add the garlic, salt and pepper, and gradually add the olive oil until the paste becomes a soft spread. Serve chilled or at room temperature, drizzled with extra virgin olive oil.

< Walnut skordalia

This version is another winner. The Macedonians came up with the addition of walnuts, but if you're not a fan try it with any nuts you like – almonds or pine nuts are especially good. I usually add more garlic, but have toned it down a bit here.

½ cup walnuts
1 cup stale Vienna or country-style sourdough bread, crusts removed
4 cloves garlic, crushed
3 tablespoons extra virgin olive oil, plus extra for drizzling
1 tablespoon red wine vinegar
2 tablespoons lemon juice

Makes 1 cup

Place the walnuts in a frying pan over high heat and toast for about 5 minutes until golden. Toss them regularly so they don't catch and burn. Transfer to some kitchen paper and cool to room temperature.

Soak the bread in a bowl of water until softened. Remove and squeeze out any excess water.

Place the bread in a blender and process until it has formed crumbs. Add the garlic and walnuts and process until the mixture looks like meal. Continue to blend while gradually adding the olive oil, vinegar and lemon juice. If the mixture is too thick, add a little more water. Serve chilled or at room temperature, drizzled with extra virgin olive oil.

Kalamata olive bread

I enjoy nothing more than waking up early on a Saturday morning and baking some fresh bread. I usually combine all the ingredients and leave the dough to rise while I go for my morning walk. Kneading the dough reminds me of my grandmother, who used to get up early every morning to make fresh bread for breakfast.

A Greek dinner table would not be complete without bread, and Greeks enjoy different breads baked for different occasions. Whatever type of bread it is, it's always accompanied by some extra virgin olive oil for dipping, into which I like to sprinkle wild oregano. In this recipe I have used some spelt flour – one of the grains used in ancient Greece.

500 g wholemeal self-raising
    flour
500 g spelt flour
½ teaspoon sea salt
½ teaspoon sugar
2 × 7 g sachets dry yeast
approximately 1½–2 cups
    warm water
extra virgin olive oil, for
    pan-frying and brushing
1 red onion, finely chopped
1 tablespoon thyme-infused
    honey
¾ cup pitted Kalamata olives,
    roughly chopped
1 tablespoon poppy seeds

Makes 1 large loaf

Sift the flours into a large bowl, reserving ½ cup of flour for rolling. Stir in the salt and sugar. Make a well in the middle. Dissolve the yeast in ½ cup warm water and pour into the well. Cover the bowl and leave to stand for 5 minutes.

Add a further cup warm water to the well and mix the yeast in well. Then slowly combine with the flour, adding little bits of water and mixing with your hands until a firm dough is formed. Flour the surface and knead the dough for at least 10 minutes, using your hands – not an electric mixer or bread maker.

Cover the bowl lightly with a tea towel and set aside for at least an hour until the dough has almost doubled in size.

Heat a little olive oil in a frying pan and cook the onion, stirring, until it just starts to caramelise. Add the honey and continue to cook, stirring, until the onion has caramelised. Remove the pan from the heat and leave to cool.

Line a baking tray with baking paper. Flatten out the dough and add the olives and caramelised onions. Knead again for about 5 minutes, then form the dough into a ball and place it on the baking tray. Cover with a tea towel and leave for another 30 minutes. Preheat the oven to 180°C.

Make a cross on the dough with a sharp knife and brush with olive oil. Sprinkle the poppy seeds over the top and bake for 30–35 minutes or until cooked and lightly golden. Serve warm.

Variations: Two other favourites of mine are saffron bread and masticha bread. Simply replace the Kalamata olives, onions and honey with either a cluster of *masticha* or a pinch of saffron infused in warm water.

Chargrilled haloumi in vine leaves

This is a great dish to add to your next barbecue. Cooking the *haloumi* in vine leaves ensures the cheese does not burn and all the flavours from the herbs and lemon juice are retained.

12 vine leaves (fresh or from
   a packet)
3 tablespoons extra virgin
   olive oil, plus extra for
   brushing
2 tablespoons lemon juice
1 teaspoon chopped oregano
1 teaspoon chopped thyme
cracked pepper
250 g *haloumi*, cut into
   6 pieces
1 lemon, cut into wedges

Makes 6

If you are using fresh vine leaves, place them in salted boiling water for 15–30 seconds, then drain. Splash with cold water to cool them down and drain again. If you are using leaves out of a packet, rinse them well in cold water to remove excess salt and drain well. Gently pat dry with kitchen paper.

Combine the olive oil, lemon juice, oregano, thyme and pepper in a bowl.

Place two vine leaves side by side so that they are overlapping. Put a piece of *haloumi* in the middle and drizzle with some of the marinade. Fold the leaves around the cheese to form a parcel. Brush with a generous amount of olive oil. Repeat with the remaining leaves, *haloumi* and marinade to make six parcels.

Place a chargrill pan or a flat grill plate over medium heat, add the parcels and cook for 2 minutes on each side.

Arrange on a plate and leave to stand for a couple of minutes, then serve hot with lemon wedges.

The vine leaf lady

Mrs Georgina Michaelides is a close family friend. I know her as 'the vine leaf lady' because she often visits my aunt and brings bags of vine leaves with her. I remember as a teenager living with my aunt, how Mrs Michaelides, huffing and puffing from her short walk up the hill to our house, often in temperatures of 30°C or more, would spontaneously appear with her bags, determined to ensure we always had fresh vine leaves for our cooking.

We would then all sit around my aunt's kitchen table and clean them, then blanch them, preparing them for when we needed to make *dolmades* (see recipe over the page). This ritual was always accompanied by Greek coffee, Greek sweets and lots of free-flowing conversation.

Mrs Michaelides was born and raised in Larnaca, a town very close to the sea in Cyprus. It's a place with strong links to the past. In the heart of modern Larnaca you will find remains of the ancient city of Kition, the birthplace of the philosopher Zenon, founder of the Stoic School.

'Living in Larnaca was the best years of my life,' says Mrs Michaelides. 'I was free and young. I could be and do whatever I wanted. I had no worries and nothing worried me.' There were five children in her family: three girls and two boys. They would regularly prepare food at home and then all walk for half an hour to sit next to the rocks by the sea, the *tsakiles* as they called them, to eat and socialise together. They would take *haloumi* cheese – a speciality of Cyprus – melons, tomatoes, olives and bread. After lunch, they would have a quick swim before returning home. Mrs Michaelides also remembers the family's regular walks to the main square to have coffee at the cake shops there and watch the people going by. At festivals and other celebrations, the townpeople would perform a local dance called the *sirto*.

Local traditions were important. One of them was to hang fresh pomegranates outside to dry so that they could be eaten during the winter months. Today, Mrs Michaelides still talks fondly of the traditional dishes for which the region of Larnaca is famous. These include the local Easter cake called *flaounes*, which is made with cheese and spiced preserved fruits in syrup. Then there's *tava*, a type of stew made with cumin, rice and pork. At Easter this would be made with lamb. Another Cypriot speciality dish is *savoro*. This is a fish similar to whiting that is floured and deep-fried. A sauce is then prepared with garlic, rosemary, red wine vinegar, flour and water, and poured over the fish. Local sausages called *loukanika* are made with pork and coriander seeds, then soaked in red wine and smoked (see recipe on page 170). Then there are the local sweet pies called *pashides*. These consist of freshly made pastry, which is rolled in olive oil and cinnamon, then deep-fried and garnished with sugar. There is also a sweet called *katimeri* made with sweet pastry and fresh homemade cream known as *shandigi*.

Mrs Michaelides came to Australia in October 1966 to join her sister and brother, and married a year later. Just as was the case for many other Greek women, her marriage was pre-arranged. She recalls arriving on the *Patris* and, while going under the Harbour Bridge, someone telling her that once they went past the bridge there would be no turning back. The ship docked at Pyrmont and she remembers making a wish for good luck and a good life.

She still has many family members in Cyprus. Many of the recipes she cooks were passed down from her family and she has also adopted other recipes that friends have shared with her. Some of her favourite recipes connect her with Cyprus. These include *endratha*, braised potatoes and lamb with a cinnamon egg and lemon sauce (see recipe on page 171); *lesmatzi*, bread made with a topping of onions, minced meat, tomato and parsley and baked in the oven; and *koupes*, parcels made with a crushed wheat mixture and filled with minced meat.

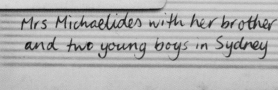

Goat and pine nut dolmades

Goat is always cooked during festivities and to celebrate special occasions, and I love to include the meat in my *dolmades*. This is my favourite recipe; however, you can use lamb instead of goat, or make a vegetarian version by leaving out the meat altogether. I prefer to use fresh vine leaves but if you can't get hold of any, packet leaves are fine – just make sure you rinse them well before use, otherwise they will be too salty. Once you've caught the *dolmade*-making bug, you'll start to do what I do: search out all your Greek neighbours. No doubt one of them will be growing vine leaves and will be happy to give you some fresh from their garden. The *dolmades* can be made in advance but are best served at room temperature.

40–50 vine leaves (fresh or from a packet)
4 tablespoons extra virgin olive oil
800 g goat's meat, cut into very small pieces
1 clove garlic, crushed
6 spring onions, finely chopped
½ cup short-grain rice
100 g pine nuts
½ cup finely chopped mint
1 cup finely chopped flat-leaf parsley
3 tablespoons finely chopped dill
sea salt and cracked pepper
½ cup white wine
½ cup water, plus extra for cooking
1 large potato, peeled and thinly sliced
2 lemons, cut into wedges
juice of 1 lemon

Makes about 40

If you are using fresh vine leaves place half the leaves in salted boiling water for 15–30 seconds, then drain. Repeat with the remaining leaves, then place all the vine leaves in a colander to drain. If you are using leaves out of a packet, rinse well in cold water to remove excess salt and drain well. Pat dry with kitchen paper.

Heat 2 tablespoons olive oil in a frying pan or skillet over medium heat and sauté the goat's meat, garlic and spring onion. Keep turning the meat so it browns on all sides. Stir in the rice, pine nuts, herbs, salt, pepper and wine, then add the water and stir gently for about 5 minutes until the liquid has evaporated. Take the pan off the heat and leave the mixture to cool to room temperature.

Layer the potato slices over the base of a large, deep saucepan to ensure the *dolmades* don't stick to the bottom.

Lay the vine leaves on a flat surface and spoon about a teaspoon of the mixture on the end where the stem begins (you may need to do this in batches). Fold the sides of the vine leaf over the filling, then firmly roll the leaf all the way up, starting at the stem end, to form a neat parcel. When you have finished making all the *dolmades*, arrange them seam-side down in tightly packed layers in the saucepan.

Pour 1–2 cups of water over the *dolmades* until the water level is about 5 mm below the top of the top layer. Drizzle with 2 tablespoons olive oil. Place a plate, face-side down, on the *dolmades* to press them down so they retain their shape and do not open up. Cover and simmer over low heat for about 1 hour until they are cooked through. The easiest way to tell is to try one – the rice should be *al dente*.

Remove the plate and pour the lemon juice over the *dolmades*. Set aside to cool. Serve on a platter with lemon wedges and a bowl of herbed yoghurt dip (see page 39).

Snails with rosemary and garlic

People don't associate snails with Greek cuisine; however, they are a predominant feature on menus in many parts of the country. It is believed that the people of Santorini were the first to consume snails, with this tradition dating back to around 10 700 BC. This is my favourite recipe for snails, inspired by my travels around Crete in 2005.

It is important to prepare and clean the snails according to the producer's instructions, and make sure they have already been purged for a period of seven days. I usually put them in the freezer for an hour before I begin cooking, then boil them for 5 minutes and plunge them into iced water to cool down. Then I repeat the process. Next I give them a quick wash and drain them well. They are then ready to cook. Once prepared, I use a toothpick to eat them, as they do in Crete.

¼ cup extra virgin olive oil
1 clove garlic, crushed
2 cloves garlic, extra, sliced
2 teaspoons roughly chopped
  rosemary
2 tablespoons red wine
  vinegar
12 snails in their shells
sea salt and cracked pepper

Makes 12

Heat the olive oil in a frying pan or skillet over low heat, add the crushed and sliced garlic and the rosemary and stir for about 1 minute. Add the vinegar, snails, salt and pepper, then cover with a lid because the oil splatters everywhere.

Cook for 10 minutes, shaking the pan and stirring regularly, until the snails are cooked. Serve immediately with some crusty bread.

Spicy ouzo keftedes stuffed with kasseri cheese

Kasseri is a Greek cheese made of goat's milk. It has a creamy, mild, sweet taste that complements the *ouzo keftedes* beautifully. It also melts a lot quicker than *haloumi* and some other Greek cheeses. Served with *tzatziki* (see page 39), these *keftedes* make a tasty addition to a *meze* plate, but they can also be eaten as a main meal with a salad. I serve them with the Santorini caper and tomato sauce (see page 92).

½ loaf stale Vienna or
   country-style sourdough
   bread, crusts removed
1 kg minced beef or lamb,
   or a combination of both
1 clove garlic, crushed
10 spring onions, finely
   chopped
1 cup finely chopped
   flat-leaf parsley
4–5 teaspoons ground cumin
a few dashes of *ouzo*
2 tablespoons extra virgin
   olive oil
1 egg
sea salt and cracked pepper
200 g *kasseri* cheese, cut into
   very small cubes
olive oil, for pan-frying

Makes about 30

Soak the bread in a bowl of water until softened. Remove and squeeze out any excess water.

Place the bread in a large bowl and add the minced meat, garlic, spring onion, parsley, cumin, *ouzo*, olive oil, egg, salt and pepper. Using your hands, mix the ingredients together well. Cover the bowl with plastic wrap and refrigerate for at least 2 hours.

Preheat the oven to 150°C.

When ready to cook, take a generous teaspoon of the mince mixture and flatten it out slightly in the palm of your hand. Add a cube of *kasseri*, then work the meat so that it forms a small ball, enclosing the cheese. Repeat with the remaining mixture and cheese, dipping your hands in water between each one to prevent sticking.

Pour olive oil into a frying pan to a depth of about 1.5 cm and set over medium heat. Add the *keftedes* in batches and lightly fry until they are golden brown. It is best not to overcrowd the frying pan, so make sure there is a little space between each one. Drain on a dish lined with kitchen paper.

Place the *keftedes* on a baking tray and bake for 5 minutes to ensure they are thoroughly cooked inside. Serve hot.

Deep-fried zucchini flowers stuffed with crab

I love the colour and unique flavour of zucchini flowers. When I decided to create a couple of recipes for them I went to the markets and bought a box of the male flowers (I prefer to cook with these as they are just the big yellow flower without the small zucchini attached). There were approximately 80 zucchini flowers in the box and I am not ashamed to say that over the course of the next four days I stuffed and ate the lot! They are extremely more-ish and in this recipe the crunchy *ouzo* batter is divine.

24 male zucchini (courgette)
   flowers
2 lemons, cut into wedges
sea salt, to serve

Batter
200 g plain flour
⅔ cup cold sparkling
   mineral water
5 ice cubes
3 tablespoons *ouzo*

Stuffing
200 g fresh crabmeat
100 g dried breadcrumbs
½ cup chopped flat-leaf
   parsley
3 tablespoons finely chopped
   spring onion
sea salt and cracked pepper

Makes 24

Clean the zucchini flowers by removing the middle yellow stamens – I usually do this with a pair of kitchen tweezers. Be careful not to tear the flowers, or crush the stamens and spread the pollen.

To make the batter, mix together the flour, water, ice cubes and *ouzo* until smooth and free of lumps. Set aside to rest while you make the stuffing.

Place the stuffing ingredients in a bowl and gently mix together.

Carefully open each zucchini flower and fill them with as much stuffing mixture as you can. Gently pinch the points of the flowers to close.

Pour olive oil into a large frying pan or wok to a depth of 3 cm and heat to 190°C (when a drop of batter dropped in the oil browns in 10 seconds). Working in batches of about four or five, dip each flower in the batter, allowing any excess to run off, and deep-fry until golden brown. Drain on kitchen paper and serve immediately with lemon wedges and a sprinkling of sea salt.

Variation: Another delicious stuffing can be made with Greek cheeses. Mix together 100 g grated *myzithra* cheese or ricotta, 100 g grated *graviera* or *kefalogaviera* cheese, 100 g crumbled Greek feta, 1 beaten egg, 3 tablespoons chopped flat-leaf parsley, 3 tablespoons chopped dill, 3 tablespoons chopped spring onion and season with sea salt and cracked pepper. Proceed with the recipe above.

Fava

Fava is a purée made from the small yellow dried split peas of Santorini. The island is renowned for the quality of its fava, which has a wonderful vibrant colour, earthy flavour and velvety texture. In the traditional Greek kitchen, favas are also made from vegetables and other pulses, such as dried broad beans (*koukofava*), white beans and giant beans. Whichever pulse you use, fava is great on its own as an appetiser or as an accompaniment to seafood.

1 cup yellow dried split peas, rinsed
3 cups water
1 onion, peeled
2 bay leaves
sea salt and cracked pepper or white pepper
3 tablespoons extra virgin olive oil, plus extra for drizzling
1 small red onion, chopped
3 tablespoons capers and/or caper leaves, rinsed and drained
1 lemon, cut into wedges

Makes 1 cup

Place the split peas, water, onion and bay leaves in a saucepan. Bring to the boil, then reduce the heat and simmer, stirring occasionally, for 45–60 minutes until the peas are soft and have cooked to a pulp. Add more water if necessary.

Discard the onion. Stir in the salt, pepper and olive oil.

To serve, drizzle with a little extra olive oil and garnish with red onion and capers. Serve with lemon wedges.

Summer watermelon soup >

We usually think of soup as a dish to be enjoyed in winter. However, in Greece we enjoy many summer soups made with a variety of fruit and vegetables, including tomatoes, cucumber, melons and, my favourite, watermelon.

4 slices *pastourma*
¼ watermelon, chilled
1–2 teaspoons ground cumin
½ cup chopped mint, plus extra to garnish
4 tablespoons extra virgin olive oil
sea salt and cracked pepper
12–16 ice cubes
4–5 tablespoons crumbled Greek feta

Serves 4

Preheat the oven to 180°C. Place the *pastourma* on a baking tray and bake for 5 minutes or until crisp. Remove from the oven and cool to room temperature, then break it up a little.

Remove the outer skin and seeds from the watermelon and chop the flesh into chunks. Place in a blender with the cumin, chopped mint, olive oil, salt and pepper and blend until smooth.

Spoon the soup into bowls, then add the ice cubes. Place a little pile of feta in the middle of each bowl, top with some *pastourma* and sprinkle with a little extra mint. Serve immediately.

< Mastic-infused prawns wrapped in kataifi pastry

Masticha (mastic chewing gum) has long been known by ancient Greeks to have healing and therapeutic properties. In this recipe, it works beautifully to highlight the delicate sweetness of the prawns and the crunchy *kataifi* pastry, which is a sort of shredded filo.

1 cup extra virgin olive oil
1 large crystal *masticha*
12 large raw prawns, peeled
   and deveined
100 g *kataifi* pastry
extra virgin olive oil, extra,
   for pan-frying

Serves 3

Pour enough olive oil into a non-stick frying pan to cover the base and set over medium heat. When the oil has heated, add the *masticha* and stir with a metal spoon until it dissolves. Remove from the heat immediately and pour into a 250 ml glass jar. Add the remaining olive oil and fill the jar to the top. Cool to room temperature.

Place the prawns in a bowl and add enough mastic oil to just cover them. Refrigerate for at least 2 or 3 hours (or overnight) so the prawns are infused with the mastic flavour.

On a clean surface lay out long strips of pastry about the same width as the prawns. Place a prawn on each strip of *kataifi* and wrap them up. Squeeze each one lightly in your hand to ensure the pastry stays together.

Heat a little extra oil in a non-stick frying pan over medium heat and cook the wrapped prawns on both sides until the pastry is crispy and golden brown. Drain on kitchen paper and serve hot.

Smoked salmon and feta parcels

In my opinion, smoked salmon served on its own can be a little dull. Combine it with a slice of feta, however, and the result is magical. When I want to turn these delicious morsels into a meal, I make a fennel and parsley salad (see page 119) and lay the parcels on top.

1 Lebanese cucumber, peeled
12 slices fresh smoked salmon
200 g Greek feta or goat's
   milk feta, thinly sliced
½ cup chopped dill
1 teaspoon red peppercorns
juice of ½ lemon
2 tablespoons extra virgin
   olive oil

Makes 12

Cut the cucumber in half, remove the seeds and cut into 1 cm wide slices.

Lay out each piece of smoked salmon and top with a slice of feta, a couple of pieces of cucumber and some dill. Roll up the salmon pieces to form parcels and place in a serving dish, seam-side down.

In a small bowl, mix together the peppercorns, lemon juice, olive oil and remaining dill. Pour over the salmon parcels and serve.

Be careful what you call 'feta'

Feta cheese is the quintessential Greek cheese whose tradition dates back thousands of years and to this day is still made by monks and shepherds in the Greek mountains. According to Greek mythology the gods sent Aristaios, son of Apollo, to teach Greeks the art of cheese making. And the Greeks learnt it well!

The Greek word *feta* means 'slice' and it is traditionally served in thin slices resting on top of a salad or by itself at the dinner table. Greek feta is made predominantly with sheep's milk and a small percentage of goat's milk. Cow's milk is never used in the production of Greek feta. In other countries where this type of cheese is made, such as Denmark, they usually use artificially blanched cow's milk. Beware – it's not the real thing.

To make feta, curdled milk is separated and allowed to drain in a special mould or a cloth bag. It is cut into large slices that are salted and then packed in barrels filled with brine.

In 2005 the European Union's highest court ruled that feta cheese is a traditional Greek product that deserves protection throughout the 27-nation bloc. As a result, non-Greek European producers are no longer permitted to call their product 'feta', which will guarantee the quality and purity of the real thing for the rest of us. This ruling was used in a similar way to disallow the use of the word 'parmesan' for any non-Italian cheese. It is crucial for maintaining the integrity of the product and making it clear to consumers just what it is they are buying. Unfortunately in Australia we still see many inferior cheeses from both European and non-European sources sold under the name 'feta'. My hope is that this will change some time in the near future.

There are many varieties of feta produced in Greece and unfortunately most of these are unavailable in Australia. Some varieties are soft and silky; others are hard and crumbly; there are tangy and salty varieties; and lemony and sour varieties. In Greece you can also purchase varieties that are infused with a variety of other ingredients such as herbs and peppers.

The biodiversity of the land in Greece, along with the varied and special breeds of sheep and goats, is what gives Greek feta the amazing and unique aromas and flavours, in my opinion. Non-Greek varieties just don't come anywhere close.

The most memorable feta I have ever had was on the island of Crete. It was when I visited a small taverna in the village of Anogeia. The feta in the salad was smooth and silky; it had salty, sour and sweet tones. Visiting shops that sold feta was also a bit of an adventure. In Crete and many other parts of Greece you can find wonderful displays of barrel-aged feta as well as feta stored in clay pots and in beautifully shaped woven baskets. The Greeks take great pride in the presentation and packaging of their renowned cheese.

I use feta every opportunity I can. I believe it is one of the most versatile cheeses in the world. As a main ingredient it finds its way into my pies, salads, fritters, pasta dishes, risottos and of course it is a staple on the *meze* table. It can be grilled or baked and even sautéed. In summer I add crumbled feta to my tomato or fruit juice, and if I am in an indulgent mood I dip cubes of feta into some melted chocolate, let it set and have it for dessert.

Pastries and pies

Pie-making in Greece began in ancient times, with layers of dough packed with salty cheese and honey, and is still an integral part of our culinary tradition. There are literally hundreds of varieties, made from meat, poultry and seafood, pulses, fruit, nuts and olives, and every vegetable imaginable. Pies are the Greek solution to fast food, and they are generally eaten as a meze, *a main meal or as a snack on the run. Here is just a small sampling of my favourites.*

Greek cheese and leek filo triangles with a dash of ouzo

Cheese triangles are one of the most well known *meze* in Greek cuisine, and here I have used a combination of Greek cheeses. If you cannot find *myzithra* or *kasseri*, use *kefalotiri* or *kefalograviera* instead.

250 g Greek feta, crumbled
250 g *myzithra* cheese, grated
150 g *kasseri* cheese, grated
3 eggs
3 tablespoons milk
cracked pepper
1 teaspoon ground nutmeg
a few dashes of *ouzo*
1 large leek, chopped
6 spring onions, chopped
½ cup chopped dill
20 sheets filo pastry
½ cup olive oil

Makes about 40

Combine the cheeses in a bowl. Beat the eggs in a separate bowl, then add the milk, pepper, nutmeg and *ouzo* and beat again. Add to the cheeses and mix with a wooden spoon, then add the leek, spring onion and dill and mix until thoroughly blended.

Preheat the oven to 150°C and line two baking trays with baking paper.

Cut the filo sheets into four equal lengths. Cover three portions with a dry tea towel so they don't dry out.

Brush one length of filo with olive oil. Cover with a second piece and brush with olive oil. Place 1½ teaspoons of the cheese mixture in the bottom right corner of the filo, leaving some space along the edge. Fold up the right corner to form a triangle and continue folding up the filo from corner to corner, until you have completed the triangle. Repeat with the remaining filo and cheese mixture.

Place the triangles seam-side down on the baking trays and brush with olive oil. Leave a little bit of room between them so that they don't stick together. Sprinkle with some water and bake for 12–15 minutes until the triangles are a light golden brown. Remove and leave to cool slightly, then serve while still hot.

A selection of pastries served as *meze*: Hellenic meat pies (top left and bottom right), Mykonean caramelised onion filo parcels (middle right) and Santorinian sweet tomato filo parcels (top right and bottom)

Hellenic meat pies

These pies (*kreatopita*) are an example of many types made on a daily basis in households all over Greece. You can replace the *haloumi* with other cheeses, such as *kefalotiri* or *kefalograviera*, and you can also use cubed meat instead of minced, if you prefer.

2 tablespoons extra virgin olive oil, plus extra for brushing
8 spring onions, finely chopped
2 cloves garlic, chopped
1 kg extra lean minced beef
sea salt and cracked paper
1 teaspoon ground cinnamon
1 teaspoon ground nutmeg
½ teaspoon ground cloves
1 cup chopped tomato
1 cup chopped flat-leaf parsley
½ cup grated Greek feta
½ cup grated *haloumi*
3 eggs
12 sheets filo pastry

Makes 12

Heat the olive oil in a frying pan or skillet over medium heat, add the onion, garlic and minced beef and cook, stirring constantly, until the meat browns. It is important that you keep mixing to break up any clumps of meat. Season with salt and pepper and stir in the ground spices. Add the chopped tomato and simmer over low heat for 5 minutes. Remove from the heat and cool to room temperature. When cool, stir in the parsley, feta, *haloumi* and eggs.

Preheat the oven to 180°C and brush 12 muffin moulds with extra virgin olive oil.

Cut the filo pastry into four long strips, then cut each strip into 5 × 5 cm squares. Place the filo squares between two clean tea towels so they do not dry out.

Line the muffin moulds with filo, brushing every second piece with olive oil. Continue until the base and sides are well covered (you will need about 12 pieces for each). Spoon the meat mixture into the moulds and season with salt and pepper. Bake for 30–35 minutes until cooked through. Serve hot.

Santorinian sweet tomato filo parcels

The abundance of Santorini's small vibrantly red, volcanically grown tomatoes inspired me to create these little parcels. The tomatoes are so juicy and tasty, having grown by the sea under the intense Cycladic sun. The only moisture they receive is from the overnight dew. I have yet to come across a tomato that shares the same aroma, earthiness and sweet flavour.

For this recipe I like to use the small grape or cherry varieties, which remind me of the small tomatoes of Santorini. The best part of this dish is pinching the tomatoes to release the pulp!

extra virgin olive oil, for
    brushing
400 g small tomatoes (use
    grape or cherry tomatoes,
    or both)
½ cup finely chopped spring
    onion or red onion
3 tablespoons chopped mint
3 tablespoons chopped basil
3 tablespoons chopped
    flat-leaf parsley
1 teaspoon dried oregano
    or thyme
sea salt and cracked pepper
200 g Greek feta, crumbled
2 eggs, beaten
6–8 sheets filo pastry

Makes 6

Preheat the oven to 180°C and brush six muffin moulds with extra virgin olive oil.

Rinse the tomatoes well and dry them. Place in a large bowl and pinch them so that the pulp comes out. Add the onion, herbs, salt, and pepper and mix well. Stir in the feta and beaten egg.

Cut the filo pastry into four long strips, then cut each strip into 5 × 5 cm squares. Place the filo squares between two clean tea towels so they do not dry out.

Line the muffin moulds with filo, brushing every second piece with olive oil. Continue until the base and sides are well covered (you will need about 12 pieces for each). Spoon the tomato mixture into the moulds and season with salt and pepper. Bake for 30–35 minutes until cooked through. Serve hot.

Mykonean caramelised onion filo parcels

In Mykonos, they use onion in their pies. I have come up with my own interpretation, where they look like gorgeous flowers when they come out of the oven.

2 tablespoons extra virgin
   olive oil, plus extra for
   brushing
8 red onions, finely chopped
2 teaspoons finely chopped
   rosemary
2 teaspoons finely chopped
   thyme
sea salt and cracked pepper
1 tablespoon thyme-infused
   honey
200 g grated Greek feta
2 eggs, lightly beaten
12 sheets filo pastry

Makes 12

Heat the olive oil in a large frying pan over medium heat, add the onion and cook, stirring, for 2–3 minutes. Add the herbs, salt, pepper and honey and cook, stirring, for a further 5 minutes until the onion has caramelised. Transfer to a bowl and leave to cool to room temperature.

When the mixture has cooled, drain off any liquid and add the feta and beaten egg. Mix well.

Cut the filo pastry into four long strips, then cut each strip into 5 × 5 cm squares. Place the filo squares between two clean tea towels so they do not dry out.

Preheat the oven to 180°C and brush 12 muffin moulds with extra virgin olive oil.

Line the muffin moulds with filo, brushing every second piece with olive oil. Continue until the base and sides are well covered (you will need about 12 pieces for each). Spoon the caramelised onion mixture into the moulds and season with salt and pepper. Bake for 30–35 minutes, then serve while still hot.

Prawn and scallop filo 'karameles'

I have given this dish its name because I twist the filo pastry to form the shape of Greek *karameles* (lollies), though you can make whatever shape you like. Serve them with herbed yoghurt dip (see page 39) and a green salad.

250 g raw prawns, peeled
   and deveined
8 scallops, with roe
4 tablespoons extra virgin
   olive oil, plus extra for
   brushing
½ teaspoon dried wild
   oregano
sea salt and cracked pepper
1 clove garlic, crushed
1 small fennel bulb,
   finely chopped
6 spring onions,
   finely chopped
3 tablespoons chopped
   flat-leaf parsley
3 tablespoons chopped dill
3 tablespoons chopped tomato
100 ml fresh cream
1 pinch saffron
8 sheets filo pastry

Serves 4

Place the prawns and scallops in a bowl, add 2 tablespoons of the olive oil, the oregano and a little salt and pepper and toss to combine.

Heat an oiled chargrill pan and sear the prawns and scallops for 1–2 minutes on each side. Set aside.

Heat the remaining olive oil in a skillet or frying pan, add the garlic, fennel and spring onion and sauté for a couple of minutes. Stir in the parsley, dill and tomato, season with salt and pepper and cook for 2 minutes.

In a separate pan, heat the cream and add the saffron. Pour into the vegetable mixture and mix well.

Remove the pan from the heat and add the prawns and scallops. Transfer to a bowl and cool to room temperature.

Preheat the oven to 150°C and line a baking tray with baking paper.

Take one sheet of filo pastry and brush with extra virgin olive oil. Place a second sheet on top and brush with olive oil (cover the remaining sheets with a dry tea towel to prevent them drying out). Spoon a quarter of the prawn and scallop mixture onto one of the corners, then carefully roll up the parcel diagonally. Twist the ends to form the shape of a lolly or cracker.

Repeat to make four parcels and place on the baking tray. Brush the tops with olive oil and bake for 25–30 minutes or until golden brown. Serve hot.

Lamb filo parcels (middle), and Greek cheese and leek filo triangles with a dash of ouzo (behind)

Lamb filo parcels

I love filo pastry. When I am unsure of what to cook, I toss together all the ingredients I have in the fridge (in this case, leftover baked lamb) and wrap them up in filo. A few minutes later I have a meal made in heaven! These parcels are main-meal size, but you can make smaller ones in any shape for a *meze*.

2 tablespoons extra virgin
  olive oil, plus extra for
  brushing
1 red onion, finely chopped
2 cloves garlic, crushed
1 carrot, finely chopped
2 bay leaves
500 g cooked lamb rump,
  trimmed and finely diced
1 teaspoon chopped thyme
sea salt and cracked pepper
1 tomato, finely chopped
3 tablespoons red wine
  (I use merlot)
1 cup chopped flat-leaf parsley
2 tablespoons double cream
100 g Greek feta, crumbled
  or grated
8 sheets filo pastry

Serves 4

Heat the olive oil in a skillet or frying pan over medium heat and sauté the onion, garlic, carrot and bay leaves for a couple of minutes. Add the diced lamb, thyme, salt and pepper and cook until lightly browned, stirring the meat to avoid clumping.

Add the tomato and wine, reduce the heat and simmer for about 15 minutes until almost all the liquid has evaporated.

Remove from the heat and discard the bay leaves. Stir in the parsley and cream, then set aside to cool to room temperature. Once cool, mix in the feta and divide the mixture into four portions.

Preheat the oven to 150°C. Lightly oil a baking tray or line with baking paper.

Place one sheet of filo flat on a clean work surface and brush lightly with olive oil. Place a second sheet on top and brush again. Spoon one portion of the lamb mixture onto one end of the filo and fold the bottom edge of pastry over the filling. Fold in the two sides, and roll up to make a firm neat parcel. Place on the baking tray seam-side down and brush with olive oil. Repeat with the remaining pastry and filling to make four parcels. (Remember to cover the filo sheets you are not using with a damp tea towel to stop them drying out – any leftover pastry should be rewrapped tightly and refrigerated.)

Sprinkle the parcels with water and bake for 20–25 minutes or until they turn a deep golden brown.

Vegetable dishes

When I first started thinking about recipes for this book, the ones that stood out as really special were the vegetarian ones. While I was growing up on the island of Psara, my diet was naturally influenced by local produce and therefore consisted predominantly of pulses, seafood, fruit and vegetables. Of equal importance was our Greek Orthodox faith, which generally means fasting on Wednesdays and Fridays and on other important religious occasions (fasting takes up at least half the year). On these days, certain foods such as meat, fish, milk and eggs must be abstained from. But as you will see from the recipes that follow, this is no great hardship.

Mushrooms with ouzo and basil

Greek people love their mushrooms, particularly in the regions of Garavene and Kastraki, where hundreds of varieties are said to grow wild. This rich bounty is quickly turned into mushroom sauces and pies, pickled or added to meat dishes.

This recipe is very quick to make and absolutely delicious, on its own or as an accompaniment to meat. I love the aniseed taste of the *ouzo* and the way it complements the earthy mushrooms and the sweet aroma of basil. You can use any type of mushroom you like, or a combination.

300 g button mushrooms
2 tablespoons extra virgin
    olive oil
sea salt and cracked pepper
2 tablespoons *ouzo*
½ cup finely chopped basil

Serves 2

Clean and peel the mushrooms, then cut them in half. If you are using larger ones, slice them thinly. Heat the olive oil in a skillet, frying pan or wok. Add the mushrooms, season to taste and toss over low heat until they are cooked and moist. Remove the pan from the heat and gently toss through the *ouzo*.

Spoon the mushrooms onto a serving platter, sprinkle with the basil and serve immediately.

Country-style baby eggplants >

In Greek cooking we like to stuff things, and this time it's baby eggplants. This is a traditional dish that my aunt Stavroula passed on to me; however, I have added a couple of extra ingredients – cinnamon and leek. Fabulous on its own or as a side, it's a very easy dish to make.

12 small baby eggplants
    (aubergines), washed
8 cloves garlic, thinly sliced
10 spring onions, finely
    chopped
2 cups chopped flat-leaf
    parsley
sea salt and cracked pepper
1 leek, finely chopped
1½ cups tomato purée (from
    fresh tomatoes)
1 teaspoon ground cinnamon
3–6 tablespoons extra virgin
    olive oil

Serves 4

Preheat the oven to 180°C.

Make a fine slit down the length of each eggplant. Take care as you don't want to cut the eggplants in half, and make sure you leave about 1 cm uncut at each end so they will hold together when stuffed.

Stuff each eggplant with two or three slices of garlic and a little spring onion and parsley, reserving some for later. Carefully place the eggplants in a baking dish with the stuffed sides facing upwards. Season with salt and pepper and scatter with the remaining garlic, spring onion and parsley.

Add the chopped leek, then the tomato purée and season again with salt and pepper as well as the cinnamon. Drizzle the olive oil over the top and bake for 25–30 minutes, or until the eggplants are nice and soft. Serve hot or at room temperature.

Baked fennel with myzithra and oregano

Fennel is another one of my favourite flavours. I enjoy it thinly sliced and tossed with rocket in a salad, or stuffed and baked in the oven; it's fabulous in seafood dishes or with goat or lamb. There is no limit to what you can do. Here is a recipe that will complement any seafood or meat dish. If you are unable to find *myzithra* you can use *kefalotiri* or *kefalograviera*.

4 baby fennel bulbs, trimmed
100 ml extra virgin olive oil
50 g *myzithra* cheese, grated
1–2 cloves garlic, finely
    chopped
1 teaspoon dried wild oregano
sea salt and cracked pepper
½ cup fresh cream
1 lemon, cut into wedges

Serves 2

Place the fennel bulbs in a saucepan of salted water and cook over medium heat for 15–20 minutes until softened. Drain and leave to cool for 10 minutes.

Preheat the oven to 180°C. Brush a baking dish with a little olive oil.

Cut the fennel into 1 cm thick slices and layer them around the dish. Sprinkle the *myzithra* over the top.

In a frying pan or skillet, combine the garlic, oregano, salt, pepper and remaining olive oil and cook for 1 minute to infuse all the flavours. Pour evenly over the fennel, then add the cream. Bake for about 20 minutes, then serve with lemon wedges.

Santorini caper and tomato sauce

This sauce is native to Santorini and makes great use of its local produce. I first tasted it when I dined at Selene, one of my favourite restaurants on the island. It works well with any seafood dish, but I especially like it with deep-fried sardines.

2 tablespoons extra virgin
    olive oil
1 red onion, finely chopped
1 clove garlic, crushed
3 tablespoons sweet white
    wine
1 cup small capers, rinsed
    and drained
1 cup tomato pulp (finely
    chopped fresh tomatoes)
2 bay leaves
sea salt and cracked pepper

Makes 1 cup

Heat the olive oil in a skillet or frying pan and sauté the onion and garlic for 2–3 minutes or until softened. Add the wine, capers, tomato and bay leaves and season with salt and pepper. Simmer over low heat, stirring occasionally, for about 35 minutes until the sauce is thick and chunky, like a chutney.

Kalamata-style toutoumakia

This recipe is the way I love to cook my pasta – it's great when you are in a hurry and want to get something on the table quickly. *Toutoumakia* is the name for egg noodles in the Peloponnesus region, but if you can't find them, use any egg-based pasta.

500 g *toutoumakia* or any other type of pasta
20 small grape or roma tomatoes
1 tablespoon red wine vinegar
100–160 ml extra virgin olive oil
sea salt and cracked pepper
6 spring onions, finely chopped
3 tablespoons finely chopped red onion
20 Kalamata olives
½ teaspoon dried wild oregano
200 g Greek feta or *myzithra* cheese, crumbled or grated
½ cup chopped basil

Serves 4

Preheat the oven to 180°C.

Bring a saucepan of salted water to the boil and cook the *toutoumakia* according to the packet instructions. Do not overcook – the pasta needs to be al dente.

Meanwhile, wash the tomatoes and place them in a baking dish. Drizzle with the red wine vinegar and 2 tablespoons olive oil. Season with salt and pepper and bake for about 5 minutes until the tomatoes begin to soften. Remove from the oven.

Heat 2 tablespoons olive oil in a skillet or frying pan and sauté the spring onion and red onion over medium heat. Add the olives and season with salt and pepper. Stir in the oregano and cook for a couple of minutes. Remove from the heat, add the tomatoes and gently mix through.

Drain the pasta, then return it to the pan. Add the remaining olive oil, to taste, and mix well. Tip the pasta onto a large serving platter and pour the tomato mixture on top. Sprinkle with the feta or *myzithra* and the basil, toss gently and serve immediately.

My Aunt Stavroula's makaronopita

Makaronopita is the Greek word for pasta pie (*makaronia* means 'pasta' and *pita* means 'pie'). Every region in Greece has its own version, and this one is from Peloponnesus. Whenever my aunt had leftover pasta she would mix it with other ingredients and bake it. I have used spaghetti here, but use whatever pasta you have to hand; the same applies to the cheeses. Of course, this isn't really a vegetable dish, but vegetarians – and non-vegetarians – will adore it.

extra virgin olive oil,
  for brushing
5 eggs
300 ml fresh cream
cracked pepper
100 g fresh ricotta, crumbed
100 g Greek feta, crumbed
100 g *kefalotiri* cheese, grated
120 g macaroni, cooked
  until tender
ground nutmeg, to garnish

Serves 6

Preheat the oven to 180°C. Brush a baking dish with olive oil.

In a bowl beat the eggs and cream together. Stir in some pepper, then add all the cheeses and mix again. Add the pasta, then spoon into the baking dish and sprinkle some nutmeg over the top.

Bake for 45–60 minutes until golden brown on top. Allow it to cool a little before cutting and serving.

My Aunt Stavroula's special rice

I have lost count of how many times my aunt has been asked to share this recipe. It is colourful, simple to make and works well as a side dish with just about everything.

1 cup long-grain rice
3 tablespoons extra virgin
  olive oil
2 cups hot water
5 rashers bacon, trimmed
  and chopped
½ red capsicum (pepper),
  chopped
½ green capsicum (pepper),
  chopped
1 cup mushrooms, chopped
2 tablespoons peas, thawed
  if frozen
3 eggs
sea salt and cracked pepper
3 tablespoons chopped
  flat-leaf parsley

Serves 4

Place the rice and olive oil in a saucepan and warm for about 2 minutes, stirring constantly. Stir in the hot water. Cook until the rice is al dente, then drain and set aside.

Heat the olive oil in a frying pan or skillet and cook the bacon for 2–3 minutes until golden brown. Transfer to a large bowl.

In the same frying pan, lightly sauté the red and green capsicum so that it still has a bit of crunch. Add to the bowl with the bacon. Add the mushrooms and peas to the pan and cook for 1–2 minutes. Transfer to the same bowl.

Crack the eggs into the frying pan (you made need some extra oil) and break the yolks so the egg cooks evenly. Once cooked, transfer to a plate and chop into small pieces. Add to the bowl.

Add the rice to the bowl, season with salt and pepper and mix together well. Transfer to a serving platter and garnish with the chopped parsley.

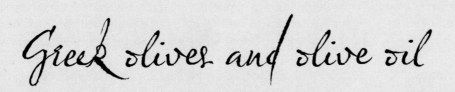

Greek olives and olive oil

Olives and olive oil are at the heart of Greek culture and cuisine. In fact, it wouldn't be going too far to say that the Greeks are obsessed with the olive – and they have been for a very long time.

Olive trees were so sacred in ancient times that anyone who cut one down was likely to be condemned to death or exiled. Winners at the first Olympic Games in 776 BC were awarded an olive branch as a sign of victory. The oil made from pressed olives was, and still is, considered 'liquid gold', as Homer described it. The oil is so much more than an ingredient in Greek cooking – it is used for medicinal purposes, in cosmetics and soap as well as to fuel the lamps in churches. It is even mixed in the cement used to build churches in some parts of Greece.

At my cooking school, Greekalicious, and at home, I use only Greek extra virgin olive oil – even for deep-fying. No other oil measures up. When people see me frying in extra virgin olive oil they gasp at the quantity I use and how costly this is. However, when it comes to health, you cannot put a price on it. I truly believe that olive oil is so much better for your health than other oils and fats. The high consumption of olive oil has been shown to be one of the main reasons the people of Crete have a low rate of heart disease and long life expectancy.

I prefer to use olive oil from Greece, especially from Kalamata and Crete. One of my favourite olive oils – and one that I use at home and at my cooking school – is an organic extra virgin olive oil made by the monks at the historic Monastery Agia Triada of Jagarolon, in Crete. The monks have been making olive oil and wine in this location since 1632 – they know what they're doing! The combination of centuries-old trees, fertile soil, healthy climate and the care and dedication of the monks gives the oil the most amazing fragrance and taste.

Deep-fried artichokes with yoghurt and walnut dip

I enjoy cooking with artichokes, not least because they are such a beautiful vegetable to look at. They are delicious with the yoghurt and walnut dip, but you could also serve them with chestnut skordalia (see page 53) for something different.

12 small artichokes
2 tablespoons lemon juice
½ cup plain flour
3–4 eggs
¾ cup dried breadcrumbs
1–2 teaspoons dried wild
    oregano
sea salt and cracked pepper
olive oil, for pan-frying
sea salt flakes, to serve
1 lemon, cut into wedges

Yoghurt and walnut dip
1 cup walnuts, toasted and
    chopped
1 cup Greek-style yoghurt
2 cloves garlic, crushed
juice of ½ lemon
3 tablespoons extra virgin
    olive oil
2 tablespoons chopped
    flat-leaf parsley, plus extra
    to garnish
sea salt and cracked pepper

Serves 4

To make the dip, place the walnuts in a blender and process for 1 minute. Add the yoghurt and garlic and process for a further minute, then add the lemon juice, olive oil, parsley, salt and pepper and process for 30 seconds. Transfer to a bowl and refrigerate for at least 1 hour. Garnish with a little extra parsley before serving.

Cut the stalks off the base of the artichokes and remove three to four layers of the tough outer leaves until you are left with the softer inner layers. Slice about 2.5 cm off the top and scoop out the furry centre, which is above the heart. Cut the artichokes in half.

Fill a bowl with water and add the lemon juice. Place the prepared artichokes in the bowl of lemon water to stop them going brown.

Arrange three bowls on your bench: place the flour in one; crack the eggs into the second bowl and whisk lightly; and in the third bowl combine the breadcrumbs, oregano and some salt and pepper.

Drain the artichokes and pat dry.

Pour olive oil into a frying pan, skillet or deep-fryer to a depth of 3 cm and set over medium heat.

Dip each artichoke in the flour, then in the egg, then coat with the breadcrumb mixture, shaking off any excess. Add to the pan and cook until the artichokes are golden brown. Drain on kitchen paper.

Arrange the artichokes on a serving platter and sprinkle with a few sea salt flakes. Serve with the walnut dip and lemon wedges.

< Baked asparagus with oregano, feta and lemon zest

To the ancient Greeks, asparagus represented the spear of love. Here it is simply combined with feta, garlic and lemon. Eat it as a main meal or serve it as an accompaniment to meat or poultry. When available, I like to mix the green, purple and white varieties because they look so beautiful together.

2 bunches asparagus
sea salt and cracked pepper
100 g feta, crumbled
4 tablespoons extra virgin
   olive oil
2 cloves garlic, crushed
2 tablespoons grated
   lemon zest
1 teaspoon dried wild oregano
juice of 1 lemon
1 tablespoon chopped dill
   (optional)

Serves 4

Preheat the oven to 180°C.

Wash the asparagus and place in a baking dish. Season with salt and pepper, then scatter the crumbled feta over the top.

Heat the olive oil in a frying pan or skillet over low heat, add the garlic, lemon zest and oregano and cook, stirring, until the garlic is lightly golden. Remove the pan from the heat, stir in the lemon juice and pour over the asparagus and feta.

Bake for 15 minutes or until the asparagus is tender. Garnish with dill (if using) and serve.

Zucchini stuffed with kopanisti

Kopanisti cheese is made in Mykonos – it has the texture of ricotta but the sharpness of blue cheese. Unfortunately you can't buy it in Australia so I have created my own version for this recipe by combining blue cheese with ricotta.

4 large zucchini (courgettes),
   washed
200 g fresh ricotta
80 g good-quality blue cheese,
   crumbled
1 tablespoon chopped dill
cracked pepper
extra virgin olive oil, for
   drizzling

Serves 4

Preheat the oven to 200°C.

Cut the zucchini in half and remove the seeds with a spoon. Place them in a baking dish.

Combine the cheeses, dill and cracked pepper and spoon into the zucchini shells. Drizzle over some olive oil. Bake for 20–25 minutes until the zucchini are cooked but still have a slight crunch. Do not overcook them or they will become soft and watery. Serve immediately.

Greek-style grilled vegetables with caper and myzithra sauce

I have chosen red capsicum, zucchini and eggplant for this recipe simply because I love the combination, but you can use any vegetables you like. The caper and *myzithra* sauce adds an extra dimension to what initally appears to be a very plain peasant-style dish. If you can't find *myzithra*, use *kefalotiri*, *kefalograviera* or feta. I also like this dish cold the next day, as part of a *meze* plate. If you do plan to eat it the next day, keep the sauce in a separate bowl and spoon it over the vegetables when you're ready to serve.

2 red capsicums (peppers)
2 zucchini (courgettes)
1 baby fennel bulb
1 large eggplant (aubergine)
1 clove garlic, crushed
1 teaspoon dried oregano
sea salt and cracked pepper
4–5 tablespoons olive oil
1 tablespoon chopped basil

Sauce
¾ cup capers, rinsed and
    drained
1 tablespoon red wine vinegar
3 tablespoons extra virgin
    olive oil
3 tablespoons chopped
    myzithra cheese
8 large basil leaves
cracked pepper

Serves 4

Wash the vegetables and pat dry. Cut each capsicum into four pieces, and thinly slice the zucchini, fennel and eggplant. Place all the vegetables in a bowl.

Combine the garlic, oregano, salt, pepper and olive oil in a small bowl. Pour the dressing over the vegetables and toss through. Heat a well-oiled chargrill pan to hot, add the vegetables and cook on both sides until they have softened and turned slightly brown.

To make the sauce, place all the ingredients in a blender and process for 1–2 minutes.

Remove the skin from the red capsicums, then arrange the vegetables on a platter. Spoon the sauce over the top and garnish with chopped basil. Serve immediately.

< My favourite baked potatoes

This is the way I like to eat my potatoes. Serve them on their own or as a side dish with meat and poultry. The feta is optional.

1 kg potatoes, peeled and
  cut in half
sea salt and cracked pepper
3 tablespoons chopped
  rosemary
3 tablespoons extra virgin
  olive oil
50 g Greek feta, crumbled
  (optional)

Serves 4

Preheat the oven to 180°C.

Place the potatoes in a saucepan of salted boiling water and simmer for 10–15 minutes until they are slightly soft. Drain and place in a baking dish. Use a fork to break them up a little into rustic shapes.

Sprinkle with salt, pepper and rosemary and drizzle with the olive oil. Bake for 30–35 minutes or until golden brown, turning them occasionally so they cook evenly. About 10 minutes before they have finished cooking, scatter on the crumbled feta (if using). Serve hot.

Baked pumpkin with feta and pine nuts

The flavours of pumpkin, feta and pine nuts work together so well. Sometimes I add fine slices of *pastourma* to this dish, about 10 minutes before the end of the cooking time – it adds a wonderful peppery flavour that complements the sweet pumpkin and salty feta.

1 kg pumpkin, peeled and
  cut into small pieces
sea salt and cracked pepper
2 tablespoons extra virgin
  olive oil
1 teaspoon chopped rosemary
50 g pine nuts
80 g Greek feta, crumbled

Serves 4

Preheat the oven to 180°C.

Place the pumpkin in a bowl and season with salt and pepper. Add the olive oil and rosemary and mix through. Transfer to a baking dish, sprinkle the pine nuts and feta over the top and bake for 20–25 minutes until the pumpkin is tender.

Spanakopita

The art of making pies is an integral part of Greece's culinary tradition. There is a pie in Greece made from every vegetable you can think of, as well as pies with meats, poultry and, of course, olives.

Perhaps the most popular of all the Greek pies, however, is *spanakopita* (spinach pie). In Greece it is often made with wild greens. I use English spinach rather than silverbeet to give my *spanakopita* a sweeter, more delicate flavour.

2 tablespoons extra virgin
  olive oil, plus extra for
  brushing
10 spring onions, chopped
1 leek, finely chopped
2 bunches English spinach,
  washed well
1 cup chopped dill
200 g Greek feta, crumbled
sea salt and cracked pepper
2 eggs, lightly beaten
24 sheets filo pastry

Serves about 8

Preheat the oven to 200°C.

Heat the olive oil in a frying pan over medium heat and cook the spring onion and leek for 2 minutes until softened and the leek is golden. Transfer the mixture to a bowl and cool to room temperature.

Add the spinach to the pan and cook until wilted. Place the spinach in a colander with a bowl underneath, press it down with the back of a spoon, and let it drain and cool to room temperature.

Add the dill and crumbled feta to the leek and onion mixture and season with salt and pepper. Add the beaten egg and mix until combined, then stir in the spinach.

Brush a baking dish with olive oil and line the base with two sheets of filo. Brush with olive oil. Continue layering and brushing the filo every second sheet until you have used 10 sheets of pastry, allowing some to hang over the sides (cover the remaining sheets with a tea towel to prevent them drying out). Spoon the spinach mixture onto the filo base and smooth the surface with the back of the spoon.

Place a sheet of filo on top, then fold in the sides of the other filo sheets to completely cover the mixture and brush with olive oil. Continue layering and brushing the remaining sheets of filo, then push them down the side of the dish. Score the top layers of pastry into the desired number of pieces.

Sprinkle with a little water and bake for 45–50 minutes until the pastry is golden brown. Rest for 10 minutes before serving. This dish is also great the next day, served at room temperature.

From left to right: Aristea's cousin Constantina,
younger sister Elpida (the Greek word for hope),
mother Eleni and Aristea, at home in Etoloakarnania

The mountains of Etoloakarnania

Mrs Katsenos and her packet of biscuits

Mrs Aristea Katsenos is one of my aunt Stavroula's dearest and closest friends. They shop together; they cook together; they share their recipes and stories.

Mrs Katsenos was born in Etoloakarnania. This prefecture occupies the western portion of Central Greece and is surrounded by mountains. It was known for its production of olives and tobacco. There were many local festivals and celebrations to attend in Etoloakarnania. The best-known was the celebration for Saint Vlassiou, which is held on 17 August every year. Mrs Katsenos loved this day and longed for it to come quickly. She would save all her '5 cent pieces' to spend on this festive day. At the celebrations there was a man who would make a sweet called *kokorakia*. This was a toffee lollipop shaped like a rooster. Mrs Katsenos would spend all the money she had saved during the year to buy as many lollipops as she could. She would then consume one a day until she ran out.

For most of the time she spent in Greece, Mrs Katsenos's mother was very ill. Later Mrs Katsenos's sister Elpida became ill at the age of eight. These were very difficult and unhappy times for her. She had to look after the family and had sole responsibility for the many household duties.

'I remember making my own outdoor oven in Greece so that we could do all our cooking. I was fifteen years old. I was very proud of my oven. Everyone in the village wanted me to make one for them,' says Mrs Katsenos.

She used the rocks and mud that surrounded their house and moulded some steel to make the door.

In early 1964 her cousin, who was living in Australia, invited her to come out to join her. Mrs Katsenos's family was very poor and she could not see a future in Greece, so she felt she had no choice but to take up the invitation to go to Australia. She came out on the ship *Patris* with her few personal belongings all tightly packed in a single suitcase.

At the first port of call she saw a $1 bill and picked it up. She was very excited and thought to herself, 'I have not yet arrived at my destination and already I have started to make money.' She took this as a good omen.

Arriving on Easter day, 1964, Mrs Katsenos was very keen to find work. Her first job was at the Masterfoods factory. After working there briefly she left to pursue her interest in sewing and commenced work in a pillow factory. A lady would fill the pillows generously with cotton and Mrs Katsenos would then sew them neatly. It was very hard work and long hours. During lunch another lady at the factory would teach her English.

Mrs Katsenos worked very hard; she observed that she worked harder then some of the other ladies who were performing the same task as her. She approached her manager and asked him for a pay rise. He said that he could not pay her any more and she bravely resigned. The next day she found work at a factory near Hyde Park. She sewed various styles of dresses and she was paid 20 cents per finished dress.

Mrs Katsenos recalls her first purchases were a packet of biscuits and a watch that cost $22. She had never eaten a biscuit before and she had never previously owned a watch.

Mrs Katsenos still gets nostalgic for Greece and misses her family. She pines for the beautiful mountains back home and her oven. She cooks many traditional dishes and has learnt many more from her daughter's godmother, Zoi. She also cooks non-Greek dishes that she has learnt here from her friends.

Mrs Katsenos's wild green pie

In Greece this pie would be made with wild greens gathered from the mountains, and would also include poppy flowers and stems. Many Greeks living in Australia grow some type of wild greens in their backyard, but for this recipe Mrs Katsenos uses silverbeet and English spinach, both of which are widely available here.

Filling
1 bunch English spinach,
   washed well and roughly
   chopped
½ bunch silverbeet, washed
   well and roughly chopped
salt, for sprinkling
1 cup plain flour
sea salt and cracked pepper
10 spring onions, chopped
2 white onions, finely grated
2 cups chopped dill

Pastry
6 cups plain flour, plus extra
   for sprinkling
pinch of salt
1 cup extra virgin olive oil,
   plus extra for brushing
approximately 2 cups warm
   water

Serves 4–6

Place the spinach and silverbeet in a large bowl and sprinkle with some salt. Leave for 5 minutes, then squeeze the spinach and silverbeet to remove the excess liquid and transfer to another large bowl. Add the flour, salt and pepper and mix well. Add the spring onion, white onion and dill and stir until well combined. Set aside while you make the pastry.

Place the flour and salt in a large bowl and make a well in the centre. Pour the olive oil and some of the warm water into the well and begin to blend in the flour. Continue to add warm water until the mixture has a dough-like consistency. Cover the bowl and set aside in a warm place for 30 minutes.

Preheat the oven to 200°C. Brush a large baking dish with olive oil.

Turn out the dough onto a clean floured surface and knead for about 5 minutes. Divide the dough into four even pieces and knead each piece well, sprinkling the surface with a little flour as needed. Using a rolling pin, roll out each piece very thinly until it is almost double the size of the baking dish. As you finish each sheet, brush the top side with olive oil and layer them one on top of the other. Cover with a damp tea towel so they don't dry out.

Place one sheet of filo on the bottom of the baking dish, then crinkle it up so that it forms waves and fits within the dish. Brush with olive oil. Place another sheet on top – but this time let it hang over one side of the dish. Brush with olive oil. The two sheets should cover the base of the baking dish.

Spoon the filling onto the filo base. Place another sheet of filo on top, then fold in the sides of the other filo sheets to completely cover the mixture. Brush with olive oil. Place the final pastry sheet on top, creating the same wavy, crinkled effect, and tuck it down the sides of the dish. Brush with olive oil.

Sprinkle with a little water and bake for about 15 minutes or until the filo turns golden brown, then reduce the heat to 150°C and cook for a further 45 minutes. Serve hot. This dish is also great the next day, served at room temperature.

Greek-style lentil soup

This is a great winter dish to keep you warm and healthy, and is also lovely eaten the next day at room temperature. I usually add a few dashes of red wine vinegar just before serving, to give a bit of zing. This trick seems to have been passed down from ancient times, when vinegar was commonly used as a flavouring for lentil soup. Sometimes I also stir in a seeded small red chilli to spice it up a little.

250 g lentils
6 cups water
1 tablespoon olive oil
2 bay leaves
6 cloves garlic, chopped
2 large carrots, finely chopped
1 white onion, chopped
1 leek, chopped
4 tomatoes, chopped
1 cup chopped flat-leaf parsley
sea salt and cracked pepper
red wine vinegar, to serve

Serves 4

Wash the lentils, place in a saucepan and add just enough water to cover. Simmer gently for 2–3 minutes, then drain and rinse again.

Transfer the lentils to a clean saucepan and add the water and olive oil. Bring to a simmer, then add the remaining ingredients, except the vinegar. Reduce the heat to low and simmer, covered, for 25–30 minutes until the lentils are tender, stirring occasionally.

Ladle the soup into bowls and add a couple of dashes of red wine vinegar to each bowl. Serve immediately.

All-purpose Hellenic seasoning

This can be used as a seasoning for fish, meat, poultry and vegetables, or to season the barbecue. You can vary the flavour by replacing the oregano with fresh rosemary. The seasoning can be made in advance and stored in an airtight container until ready to use.

1 cup good-quality sea salt
3 tablespoons roughly
   chopped oregano
grated zest of 2 lemons

Makes 1 cup

Place all the ingredients in a mortar and pestle and grind it to a fine salt. Rub the mixture into meat or fish or sprinkle over vegetables.

If you wish to keep it in the cupboard for a few weeks then it is best to dry it out first. To do this, preheat the oven to 150°C and line a baking tray with baking paper. Spread the seasoning evenly across the tray and bake for about 30 minutes or until the herbs and lemon zest dry out. Cool to room temperature and store in a sterilised airtight container.

Seafood

After vegetables and pulses, seafood would have to be the most consumed sort of produce on the Greek menu. Greece is fortunate to be surrounded by water, which means there's a year-round abundance of fresh seafood: fish of all shapes and sizes, mussels, squid, prawns, oysters, octopus, sea urchins . . . . the list goes on. At most restaurants you can choose which item of seafood you would like to have cooked for you – it is all on display and freshly caught that day. You can quite literally see, smell and feel the freshness. I find this extremely invigorating.

There is a Greek saying that goes, 'A fish begins to stink from the head down.' The freshness of the fish can indeed be judged from the condition of its head. If the head doesn't look fresh, then the rest won't be either. I always follow this rule when purchasing seafood.

Swordfish souvlakia with fennel and parsley salad

When ancient Greeks sacrificed animals to the gods the ritual was carried out with a sword. The sacrificial meat would then be cooked and offered for consumption off the sword. The Greek word *souvla* means both skewer and sword, so when you consume a *souvlakia* you are eating a 'little sword'. Traditionally *souvlakia* are cooked with meat and vegetables, but I also really enjoy them made with seafood – use any kind of fish, prawns, octopus or mussels.

You may be surprised to see fish sauce used in the recipe, something that is usually associated with Asian cooking. However, the ancient Greeks used to manufacture a liquid from fermented fish called *garos* and it was one of the main sauces used in ancient times. It doesn't feature in many Greek dishes today, but I still find opportunities to use it when I want to add a salty element to a sauce or marinade.

4 tablespoons fennel seeds
1 kg swordfish, skin removed
   and cut into cubes
grated zest of 2 lemons
1–2 teaspoons fish sauce
cracked pepper
5 tablespoons extra virgin
   olive oil
1 lemon, cut into wedges

Fennel and parsley salad
1 baby fennel bulb,
   thinly sliced
3 tablespoons flat-leaf
   parsley leaves
juice of ½ lemon
sea salt
2 tablespoons extra virgin
   olive oil

Serves 4

Gently heat a frying pan, add the fennel seeds and toss for about 30 seconds until you can smell their aroma. Place in a mortar and roughly grind with a pestle.

Place the swordfish chunks in a bowl, add the fennel seeds, lemon zest, fish sauce, cracked pepper and olive oil and mix well. Cover and marinate in the fridge for 2–3 hours.

Meanwhile, soak eight wooden skewers in water for about 1–2 hours to ensure they do not burn during cooking. Alternatively you could use metal skewers.

Thread the swordfish onto the skewers. Heat an oiled chargrill pan, add the *souvlakia* and cook for 5 minutes each side until cooked through and lightly browned.

In the meantime, make the salad. Place the fennel and parsley in a bowl, add the lemon juice, sea salt and olive oil and toss through.

Arrange the salad on a serving platter. Top with the *souvlakia* and serve with lemon wedges.

Deep-fried cumin calamari

This is an example of an ancient Greek recipe adapted to modern times; in this case, I have replaced the original shark with squid. To put this in context, I want to share with you a recipe from Archestratus, an ancient Greek cook: 'In the city of Torone you must buy belly steaks of *karkharias* [the Greek word for shark]; sprinkle them with cumin and not much salt; you will add nothing else, dear fellow, unless maybe green olive oil ... There are not many mortals who know of this divine food, nor do they desire to eat it, those that is who have the soul of a storm patrol or a locust and are scared rigid because the creature is a man-eater. But every fish likes human flesh, wherever he can get it ...'

I enjoy purchasing the whole squid and cleaning it myself but if this doesn't appeal to you, you can buy it already cleaned, and simply cut it into thin pieces. This dish can be served as a main meal or as a *meze*.

1 kg whole squid
4–5 tablespoons ground
  cumin, depending on the
  strength of the cumin
2 cups plain flour
1 teaspoon sea salt
olive oil, for deep-frying
walnut *skordalia* (see page 53),
  to serve
2 lemons, cut into wedges

Serves 4

The important thing to remember when cleaning squid is not to puncture the ink sack, which lies to the left of the eyes. First, remove the transparent spine by running your finger gently along the inside of the mantle. Then grab the head while holding the tip of the mantle and gently pull it off. The guts will also come out. Gently and carefully cut off the tentacles (above the eyes) and keep for later. Discard the rest. Remove the wings and the skin. Make an incision with a paring knife along the wings and run your finger under the wing from the tip to the base of the hood; it then peels off easily. Wash the mantle and remove any gunk inside. Cut the bottom beak off and discard. Pat the squid dry.

Once cleaned, thinly slice the squid and place in a colander with a plate underneath so that it can drain well.

Sift the cumin and flour into a bowl and mix well. Add the sea salt.

Coat the squid in the flour mixture and shake off any excess. Heat the olive oil in a deep-fryer or heavy-based saucepan to 180°C, or until a cube of bread dropped in the oil browns in 15 seconds. Add the squid in batches and cook for about 5 minutes until golden. Take care not to overcrowd the pan.

Drain on a plate lined with kitchen paper and serve hot with walnut *skordalia* and lemon wedges.

Aegina-style salmon with pistachio crust >

Located in the Saronic Gulf, the island of Aegina not only has an abundance of fresh seafood, but is also where the best pistachios in Greece are grown.

4 × 200 g pieces fresh salmon, skin on, bones removed
sea salt and cracked pepper
100 ml extra virgin olive oil
1 cup unsalted shelled pistachios
2 tablespoons grated lemon zest
4 tablespoons chopped dill
zesty pomegranate and *pastourma* salad (see page 29), to serve

Serves 4

Preheat the oven to 180°C and line a baking tray with baking paper.

Place the salmon pieces on the tray and season with salt, pepper and about 1 tablespoon of the olive oil.

Place the pistachios in a mortar and grind with the pestle until they are coarsely broken up. Add the lemon zest, dill, pepper, salt and the remaining olive oil, mix well and grind a little more.

Spoon the mixture onto the salmon pieces and spread so it forms an even crust. Bake for 20–25 minutes until the fish is cooked. Serve with zesty pomegranate and *pastourma* salad.

Kalamata salt cod salad

During Greek Orthodox fasting periods, just about everyone in Kalamata serves dishes using *bacalao*, salt cod. As the salt cod needs to soak for at least 24 hours, you will need to begin this recipe the day before.

500 g salt cod, dried and boneless
2 bay leaves
1 small red capsicum (pepper), chopped
3 tablespoons chopped spring onion
1 small tomato, chopped
½ teaspoon dried wild oregano
sea salt and cracked pepper
½ cup chopped flat-leaf parsley
3 tablespoons chopped mint
2–3 tablespoons extra virgin olive oil
1 clove garlic, crushed
2–3 tablespoons lemon juice
1 tablespoon red wine vinegar

Serves 4

Rinse the fish really well, then immerse in a bowl of cold water. Cover and refrigerate for at least 24 hours, changing the water at least five times.

Drain the fish and place in a saucepan with the bay leaves and enough water to cover the fish. Bring to the boil, then reduce the heat to low, cover and simmer gently for about 20–25 minutes until the fish is opaque and almost falls apart into large flakes.

Drain the fish and pat dry. Separate into small flakes and remove any bones or skin, then place the flakes in a bowl. Add the capsicum, spring onion, tomato, oregano, salt and pepper and toss through gently. Add the parsley and mint and toss again.

Place the olive oil, garlic, lemon juice and vinegar in a small bowl and mix well. Pour over the salt cod salad and toss gently. Transfer the salad to a platter and serve.

Squid stuffed with feta, fresh herbs and tomatoes

I was inspired to put this dish together when I was in Mykonos. I wanted to create a colourful, light dish with feta, fresh herbs and tomatoes, a combination I dearly love. This dish goes beautifully with a rocket salad.

4 medium whole squid
3 tablespoons extra virgin
   olive oil
½ teaspoon dried oregano
sea salt and cracked pepper
2 cloves garlic, crushed
1 tomato, finely chopped
3 tablespoons finely chopped
   spring onion
2 tablespoons chopped dill
2 tablespoons chopped parsley
3 tablespoons finely chopped
   mint
1 tablespoon chopped basil
3 tablespoons finely chopped
   red capsicum (pepper)
150–200 g Greek feta,
   crumbed
1 lemon, cut into wedges
rocket, to serve

Serves 4

Thoroughly clean the squid without slitting them open (see page 120 for cleaning instructions, but leave the skin on), then pat them dry and place in a bowl.

Mix together the olive oil, oregano, salt, pepper and garlic and pour over the squid. Cover with plastic wrap and marinate in the fridge for at least 3 hours, or overnight. Turn the squid pieces regularly.

Place the tomato, spring onion, dill, parsley, mint, basil, capsicum and feta in a bowl and mix well. Stuff each squid with this mixture, then thread a small skewer through the end to seal the hole.

Place the squid on a hot barbecue or oiled chargrill pan and cook for about 3–5 minutes each side until cooked through. Serve with lemon wedges on a bed of rocket.

Greek-style fish and chips

I have used john dory fillets for this dish, but you can use other types of firm white fish, such as snapper or whiting. The potato chips are sprinkled with dried wild oregano and sea salt. In Greece, most restaurants serve potato chips this way or with melted cheese such as feta. It gives the ordinary chip a lot more flavour.

4 john dory fillets
sea salt and cracked pepper
4 large potatoes, peeled and thinly sliced into french fries
olive oil, for deep-frying
1 cup flour
½ cup ice cubes
3 tablespoons *ouzo*
½ cup sparkling mineral water
2 teaspoons dried wild oregano
lemon wedges, to serve

Serves 4

Season the fish with salt and pepper and rub it in well.

Heat some olive oil in a deep-fryer, add the potato pieces and shake them occasionally so they don't stick together. Alternatively add them to a deep heavy-based saucepan or frying pan half-filled with olive oil and cook for about 5 minutes until golden brown.

Meanwhile, pour olive oil into a frying pan (or deep-fryer) to a depth of 1.5 cm and heat over medium heat.

Combine the flour, ice cubes, *ouzo*, mineral water and 1 teaspoon of the oregano in a bowl. The mixture needs to be a smooth paste, free of lumps.

Dip one fillet at a time in the batter, allowing any excess to drain off. Place the fillets in the frying pan and cook for about 3 minutes each side until the batter is golden brown and crispy.

Drain the fish and the potato chips on kitchen paper. Transfer to a platter, sprinkle with the remaining oregano and serve immediately with lemon wedges.

Octopus stifado

I could not have written this book without including an octopus recipe – it is an essential part of any Greek family's diet. My grandmother and I used to cook octopus in a variety of ways, and I so enjoyed watching the colour change from pink to a deep red. The dish I have included here is very rich and goes well with mashed potato, plain rice or crusty bread to make the most of the delicious juices. I prefer to use a large octopus for this, rather than the small ones.

Mavrodaphne is a sweet red dessert wine from Patra. If you can't find it, use a red wine such as a merlot.

1 kg octopus, cleaned
2–3 bay leaves
½ cup extra virgin olive oil
2 cloves garlic, crushed
12 very small red onions or
  golden shallots, peeled
½ bunch thyme, tied together
1 cinnamon stick
4 cloves
sea salt and cracked pepper
200 ml *mavrodaphne*
¼–½ cup water

Serves 4

Cut the octopus into quarters. Place in a saucepan with the bay leaves and bring the natural juices to a simmer. Continue to simmer over low heat, stirring occasionally, for up to 30 minutes until all the juices have evaporated. The cooking time will vary considerably depending on the octopus. Remove the bay leaves.

Push the octopus to the side of the saucepan. Increase the heat to medium, add the olive oil and garlic and cook for 30 seconds. Add the onions. Keep turning the onions and octopus so they take on a bit of colour on all sides and the onions soften a little.

Add the thyme, cinnamon stick, cloves, salt, pepper, *mavrodaphne* and enough of the water to almost cover the octopus. Bring to a low simmer and braise for 45 minutes or until the octopus is soft and tender. Serve warm.

A *tagari*, woven from sheep's wool and made on the loom the traditional way. When I was little, I would carry my pencils and food to school in a *tagari* similar to this one.

A keen little fisherperson

One day, when I was about four years old, while living on the island of Psara, my grandmother asked me to go down to the port to purchase a *barbouni* (red mullet). We were going to cook the dish known as *plaki* (see recipe over the page) – a traditional Greek dish of fish baked in the oven with herbs, onion, extra virgin olive oil, tomatoes and potatoes. I took the long way to the port because I wanted to visit my garden.

On the way to the port I always passed a location that had lots of crosses. I was never sure why they were there. I assumed that they were crosses that people had erected after they'd said a prayer. To my amazement, that day there was also a wooden box that resembled a boat. I was overjoyed and decided to borrow it and go out to sea. I resolved that I would catch the red mullet (*barbouni*) myself and save some drachmas. I wanted to impress my grandmother. She was obsessed with always having the freshest ingredients and I knew that if I brought home a *barbouni* that had just been caught she would be pleased.

I dragged the boat to the water, pushed it out and jumped in. But it sank! I could not understand why. I became extremely upset and started to cry. I could not drag the boat out of the water; it was just too heavy. A man at the beach approached me to help. He looked at me and laughed. I was not amused. He asked me where I had found the wooden box. I told him that I had found it at the place where all the crosses were, the place where people went to pray. He continued to laugh and still I could not understand why.

Of course, my little boat was actually a coffin, and the place with all the crosses was the local cemetery. I was in lots of trouble from both my stern grandmother and the priest. It took a few weeks for them to forgive me and to start to see the humorous side of the incident.

Plaki barbouni

Red mullet, or *barbouni*, featured regularly on our dinner table in Psara, and I particularly loved it when it was baked. My grandmother would always serve me the head, the most flavoursome part, and I would spend ages pulling it apart to extract all the meat, including the eyes. *Plak* was the name of the ancient Greek griddle stone that worked like a flat oven. From this we derive the English words 'plate' and 'platter', as well as other words which all still mean 'flat'. *Plaki barbouni*, therefore, is baked red mullet. This is the way I like to cook the dish at home; sometimes I also add 1–2 red chillies to the stuffing.

1–1.5 kg red mullet, scaled and gutted (ask your fishmonger to do this)
sea salt and cracked pepper
10 small potatoes, peeled and halved
approximately ½ cup extra virgin olive oil (you may need more)
3 tablespoons capers, rinsed and drained
½ cup dried breadcrumbs
1 clove garlic, crushed
2 teaspoons dried wild oregano
8 spring onions, chopped
2 cups chopped flat-leaf parsley
1 leek, chopped
8 cloves garlic, extra, thinly sliced
2 cups tomato purée (from fresh tomatoes)
12 Kalamata olives
1 lemon, cut into wedges

Serves 4

Preheat the oven to 150°C and line a baking dish with baking paper.

Clean the fish to remove any scales that may still be there, taking extra care around the head area, and pat dry. Cut a couple of large crosses on both sides of the fish, then season with salt and pepper and rub it in well. Place the fish in the baking dish.

Combine the potatoes, salt, pepper and a couple of tablespoons of olive oil in a bowl, then arrange around the red mullet.

Roughly chop the capers and place in a bowl with the breadcrumbs, crushed garlic, 1 teaspoon of the oregano, a little of the spring onion and parsley and 3–4 tablespoons olive oil. Mix to form a paste, then push the mixture into the belly and cavities of the fish.

Arrange the leek, sliced garlic and remaining spring onion over the fish, followed by the tomato purée and remaining parsley. Season with salt, pepper and the remaining oregano, and drizzle with the remaining olive oil. Finish by placing the olives on top.

Bake for 1–1½ hours until the fish and potatoes are cooked. Towards the end of the cooking time, increase the temperature to 180°C to ensure the tops of the potatoes are golden brown.

Serve the fish whole on a platter, surrounded by the potatoes, and allow everyone to help themselves. Serve with lemon wedges.

Avgotaracho, lemon and rocket macaronia

Macaronia is the Greek word for pasta and *avgotaracho* is the orange-coloured roe of mullet. This is my favourite way to serve this delicacy – I savour every mouthful.

250 g spaghetti
extra virgin olive oil,
    for drizzling
grated zest of ½ lemon
juice of 1 lemon
generous handful of rocket
½ piece of *avgotaracho*, wax
    removed, and crumbled
    with a fork

Serves 4

Bring a saucepan of salted water to the boil and cook the spaghetti according to the packet instructions. Drain well. Place the pasta in a serving bowl, drizzle with olive oil and toss to coat the pasta.

Add the lemon zest and juice and toss through, then add the rocket and *avgotaracho* and mix gently. Serve immediately.

Stuffed saffron mussels of Psara >

On the island of Psara they use fresh mussels to prepare a rice dish similar to paella. With this recipe I stuff the mussels and serve them with some crusty bread to soak up the juices. I like to use a sweet white wine, but you could replace this with good-quality fish stock if you prefer. If you can, use Greek Kozani saffron as it has a beautiful pinkish-red colour and a wonderful flavour.

2 cups water
1 kg fresh mussels, cleaned
    and debearded
2 tablespoons warm water
pinch of saffron threads
2 tablespoons olive oil
10 spring onions, chopped
½ cup arborio rice
4 tablespoons pine nuts,
    toasted
sea salt and cracked pepper
½ cup chopped flat-leaf
    parsley
2 tablespoons chopped basil
1¼ cups white wine
1 cup chopped tomato
basil leaves, extra, to garnish

Serves 4

Place the water and cleaned mussels in a saucepan and bring to a simmer. As soon as each mussel opens, remove it immediately and place on a plate. Discard any mussels that don't open.

Combine the warm water and saffron threads in a bowl.

Heat the olive oil in a frying pan or skillet and sauté the spring onion for a couple of minutes. Add the rice, pine nuts, salt and pepper and stir for 2–3 minutes. Remove from the heat and stir in the parsley, basil and saffron mixture.

Carefully stuff each mussel with a little of the mixture and close them slightly. Layer the mussels flat in a clean frying pan or skillet until the whole pan is full. Pour in the wine and scatter the chopped tomato over the top. Cover and simmer over low heat for about 20 minutes until the rice is cooked. Garnish with basil leaves and some cracked pepper and serve.

Sardines wrapped with vine leaves

I cannot picture the Greek islands without daydreaming about *sardeles* (sardines) served with wild greens or a *horiatiki* (traditional Kalamata salad; see page 7), and of course some wine. This recipe adopts the ancient Greek practice of wrapping fish in leaves before baking.

10 sardines
sea salt and cracked pepper
10 vine leaves (fresh or
  from a packet)
3 tablespoons roughly
  chopped flat-leaf parsley
1 clove garlic, crushed
½ teaspoon dried wild
  oregano
3 tablespoons chopped
  spring onion
1 tablespoon olive oil
juice of 1 lemon
extra virgin olive oil,
  for drizzling
1 lemon, cut into wedges

Serves 2

Preheat the oven to 160°C.

Scrape off the scales and gut the sardines. I keep the heads on as, in my view, this is the best part to eat, but you can remove them if you wish. Then wash the sardines well, pat dry and season with salt and pepper.

If you are using fresh vine leaves, place them in salted boiling water for 15–30 seconds, then drain. Splash with cold water to cool them down and drain again well. If you are using leaves out of a packet, rinse them well in cold water to remove excess salt and drain well. Pat dry with kitchen paper.

In a bowl mix together the parsley, garlic, oregano, spring onion and olive oil. Season with salt and pepper and spoon the mixture into the sardines (you may need to slit each fish a little more below the gills to make room for the stuffing). Wrap each fish with a vine leaf and place in a baking dish, lining them up close together.

Pour the lemon juice over the fish and drizzle with extra virgin olive oil. Bake for 25–30 minutes until cooked through. Serve hot with lemon wedges.

Sea urchin pasta

Sea urchin can be found along the coasts of Crete, Peloponnesus and the Cyclades and, of course, the island of Psara. I cannot get enough of these unusual-tasting sea creatures. I usually eat them raw, but if I feel like cooking, they team beautifully with pasta. Try it – it's a great combination.

250 g spaghetti
4 tablespoons extra virgin
  olive oil
1 clove garlic, crushed
3 tablespoons chopped
  spring onion
1 small red chilli, seeded and
  finely chopped (optional)
½–1 teaspoon chopped
  rosemary
2 tomatoes, chopped
½ cup white wine
cracked pepper
3 tablespoons double cream
½ cup chopped flat-leaf
  parsley
2 tablespoons chopped dill
80 g sea urchin roe
2 tablespoons chopped chives
  or basil
1 lemon, cut into wedges

Serves 4

Bring a saucepan of salted water to the boil and cook the pasta according to the packet instructions.

Meanwhile, heat the olive oil in a large frying pan over low heat and sauté the garlic, spring onion and chilli (if using) for a couple of minutes. Stir in the rosemary and tomato, then add the wine and cook for 5 minutes until the liquid has reduced by half. Season with pepper, pour in the cream and cook for a further 1–2 minutes. Remove from the heat and add the parsley, dill and sea urchin roe. Gently mix the ingredients together.

Drain the pasta well, add it to the frying pan and gently mix through. Transfer to a serving dish, garnish with the chopped herbs and serve with lemon wedges.

Greek Easter

For Greeks, Easter is all about celebrating the most important event of the Orthodox calendar with family and friends. It is a colourful time, when homes are decorated with painted eggs and wreaths of fragrant flowers. As ever, food is at the centre of the festivities.

Barbecued Greek-style lamb with pomegranate salsa

This is the way I enjoy lamb the most. The pomegranate symbolises many things, including fertility, love and death, and is one of the main symbols of the goddess Aphrodite. It adds a wonderful fresh flavour to this dish.

sea salt and cracked pepper
1–2 teaspoons dried wild
  oregano
handful of oregano
1–2 teaspoons dried thyme
2 teaspoons chopped thyme
3–4 teaspoons chopped
  rosemary
6 cloves garlic, crushed
grated zest and juice of 1 lemon
3 tablespoons extra virgin
  olive oil
1–1.5 kg leg of lamb, deboned,
  some of the fat trimmed off
1 lemon, extra, cut into wedges

Salsa
1 pomegranate, seeds removed
3 tablespoons finely chopped
  parsley
4 tablespoons extra virgin
  olive oil
1 teaspoon ground cumin
1 clove garlic, crushed
1 tablespoon red wine vinegar
sea salt
1 tablespoon lemon juice
grated zest of ½ lemon

Serves 4–6

Combine the salt, pepper, herbs, garlic, lemon zest and juice and olive oil. Rub all over the lamb and cook on a very hot barbecue for 25–30 minutes until golden brown on both sides and cooked to your liking. (Alternatively, bake the lamb in a preheated 180°C oven for 1½ hours.) Remove the lamb from the barbecue or oven, cover with foil and leave it to rest for about 15 minutes.

To make the salsa, combine the pomegranate seeds and parsley in a bowl. Combine the remaining ingredients in another bowl, then add to the pomegranate mixture.

Pour the salsa over the lamb and serve with lemon wedges.

Tsoureki (Greek Easter bread)

Also known as *lambropsomo*, this is a sweet brioche-style bread that is usually braided and adorned with red Easter eggs. The bread symbolises the resurrection of Christ and is traditionally eaten during the resurrection meal – a light meal consumed after the midnight Divine Liturgy on Saturday night.

The *tsoureki* has two unusual ingredients: *masticha* (Greek chewing gum) and *mahlepi* (Mediterranean wild cherries), and these aromas fill the house when you are baking. I love this bread, and really enjoy having leftover slices for breakfast, dipped in Greek coffee.

1 kg self-raising flour
¾ teaspoon sea salt
1 teaspoon ground *mahlepi*
3 clusters *masticha*, crushed
    with ¼ teaspoon sugar
1½ cups milk
2 × 7 g sachets dry yeast
150 g unsalted butter
1 cup castor sugar
4 eggs, beaten
2 dyed red eggs (see recipe
    opposite; optional)
1 egg yolk, beaten
1 tablespoon milk, extra
50 g flaked almonds

Place the flour, salt, *mahlepi* and *masticha* in a bowl and mix to combine. Make a well in the centre.

Warm up ½ cup milk. Add the yeast to the well, carefully pour the milk into the well, then cover and set aside for 10 minutes until the yeast starts to bubble.

Place the remaining milk in a saucepan with the butter and sugar and gently warm through. Mix the sugar well so that it fully dissolves.

Add the milk mixture to the flour mixture and stir to combine. Add the beaten egg and mix well. Turn out onto on a well-floured surface and knead for 15–20 minutes until the dough becomes malleable. Cover and leave to rise in a warm place until it doubles in size – this should take about 1–1½ hours.

Uncover the dough and knead for a further 5 minutes. Divide the mixture into three ropes and shape it into a large braid. Place on a baking tray. Tuck the two eggs into the braid (if using), then cover with a clean tea towel and set aside for a further 20 minutes. Preheat the oven to 170°C.

Combine the egg yolk and extra milk in a bowl and brush all over the loaf. Sprinkle with flaked almonds and bake for 45 minutes, until golden brown. Cool on a wire rack before serving.

Greek red Easter eggs

Red eggs are a vital component of any Greek Easter celebration; indeed, they are the food that breaks the Easter fast. The egg symbolises the renewal of life and the colour symbolises the blood of Christ. The cracking of the eggs among Greek Orthodox families symbolises the opening of the tomb and the resurrection of Jesus. When we break eggs together with friends and family, one person says, '*Hristos anesti*' (Christ has risen) and the other replies, '*Allithos anesti*' (truly Christ has risen). A bit of a game is also played at the same time: each person holds their egg tightly and tries to crack other people's eggs by gently hitting the points together. The person who escapes having their egg cracked is the winner and will be blessed with good luck.

When I make my eggs I like to decorate them using parsley leaves or flowers such as geraniums. I place the leaves on the egg, then take a little piece of fabric from a pair of stockings and tie it around the leaves. Then I dye the egg. The leaves prevent the dye being absorbed, leaving a beautiful leaf print on the egg. You can buy red dye from any Greek cake shop or good delicatessen.

12 fresh white eggs
red food dye or colouring
¾ cup white vinegar
olive oil, for polishing the eggs

Makes 12

Wash the eggs with a soft cloth and place carefully in a large saucepan. Fill the saucepan with enough cold water to cover the eggs and place over low heat – don't be tempted to increase the heat or the eggs will crack. Bring the water gradually to a simmer and cook the eggs for about 1 hour. Allow to cool in the pan.

Fill another large saucepan with water. Bring to the boil, then add the red dye and boil for 2–3 minutes. Reduce the heat to a low simmer and stir in the vinegar.

Carefully add the eggs to the dye solution for a couple of minutes until they turn a vibrant red colour. Remove with a spoon and place on kitchen paper. Leave the eggs to cool slightly and absorb any excess dye, then wipe them with a little olive oil and dry them off with kitchen paper.

Greek Easter eggs can also be dyed naturally. Preboil the eggs as above, then bring a saucepan of water to the boil, add one of the following natural ingredients and simmer gently for at least 20–30 minutes. Stir in the vinegar, then add the eggs and simmer very gently for no more than 2 minutes, or remove the pan from the heat and leave to soak for a longer period – the longer the eggs soak, the more intense the colour will be.

Parsley – gives a gorgeous green colour.
Beetroot bulbs – gives a vibrant red colour.
Red cabbage – gives a colour that is almost blue.
Saffron – gives a golden yellow colour.
Yellow margarita flowers – colours the eggs sunshine yellow.
Brown onion skins or carrots – gives an orange colour.
Coffee – gives a brown colour.

From left to right:
My Aunt Stavroula's famous
galaktoboureko, *koulourakia*,
and *tsoureki* (Greek Easter bread)
with Greek red Easter eggs

My Aunt Stavroula's famous galaktoboureko

Galaktoboureko is a sweet semolina mixture wrapped in filo and served with a sweet syrup. It's my favourite dessert, and my aunt is always asked to bring some whenever we visit people. Many Greek ladies have replaced their own recipe with this one!

1 cup sugar
2 litres milk
4 egg yolks
2 teaspoons vanilla essence
2 cups semolina
250 g unsalted butter
20 sheets filo pastry

Syrup
2½ cups castor sugar
4 cups water
grated zest of 1 lemon
juice of ½ lemon

Serves 10–12

Combine the sugar and 6 cups milk in a non-stick saucepan and bring to a simmer over low heat, stirring regularly.

Meanwhile, place the egg yolks and vanilla in a 250 ml measuring cup and fill to the top with cold milk. Mix well.

When the milk and sugar mixture begins to simmer, leave the heat on low and gradually add the semolina, stirring constantly so the mixture doesn't form any lumps. When it begins to thicken, stir in the cup of milk, egg and vanilla and 20 g butter. Add the remaining milk, little by little, and stir until the mixture thickens slightly and comes to a simmer. Remove from the heat and set aside. Remember to stir the mixture occasionally while you work with the filo pastry to prevent any skin or crust forming.

Preheat the oven to 180°C. Butter a large baking dish and melt the remaining butter. Take two pieces of filo, brush with melted butter and place in the baking dish. Continue until at least 10 sheets cover the base and sides of the dish.

Pour in the semolina mixture and top with two sheets of filo (remember to brush with melted butter). Fold in the sides of the filo, brush with butter and flatten to cover the top. Place two more double filo sheets on top, brush with butter and push them down the sides so that no pastry is sticking out. Continue until all the pastry sheets have been used.

With a sharp knife, gently score the filo into diamonds or squares. Bake for about 30 minutes, then reduce the temperature to 140°C and cook for a further 1–1½ hours until the pastry is a light golden brown.

Meanwhile, prepare the syrup. Combine the sugar and water in a saucepan over low heat and simmer until the sugar has dissolved. Add the lemon zest and juice and simmer gently for 10–15 minutes until the syrup thickens slightly. Remove the pan from the heat and leave to stand at room temperature while the *galaktoboureko* cooks.

Take the *galaktoboureko* out of the oven and, while still hot, pour on the syrup. Set aside until the syrup has been absorbed. Serve warm or at room temperature.

Koulourakia

Koulourakia are Greek butter cookies. They are great to make with kids and you can form them into any shape you like. There is a traditional song the children sing when rolling the dough. The translated version is: 'I'm rolling *koulourakia* with my two little hands. I will bake them in the oven; the house will smell nice.'

4½ cups self-raising flour
1 teaspoon baking powder
125 g unsalted butter, at room
   temperature
1 cup castor sugar
4 eggs, separated
1 teaspoon vanilla extract
grated zest of 1 lemon
2 egg yolks, beaten, extra

Makes about 40

Preheat the oven to 150°C and line a large baking tray with baking paper.

Sift the flour and baking powder into a mixing bowl.

Using hand-held electric beaters, cream the butter and sugar. Beat the egg yolks in a separate bowl, then add to the butter and sugar mixture.

Beat the egg whites until stiff peaks form, then fold gently into the batter. Stir in the vanilla and lemon zest, then add the flour mixture, a little at a time, to make a soft dough.

Knead the dough for 2–3 minutes. With lightly floured hands, shape the dough into your desired shapes and arrange on the prepared baking tray. The most common shapes are twists, rounds and curly letters.

Brush the biscuits with the extra egg yolk and bake for 25–30 minutes until golden brown. Cool on a wire rack.

Meat and Poultry

The ancient Greek diet was predominantly one of pulses and vegetables, with meat only being consumed when an animal was sacrificed for a festive occasion. There would be a procession before the sacrifice, then the ritual offering of some of the animal to the gods. Afterwards, there would be a feast to eat the rest of the meat. This communal eating of meat, binding people to one another, was an essential part of the sacrifice in Greek religion. This tradition of enjoying meat on festive occasions continues today (although without the animal sacrifice), with recipes made from lamb, chicken, pork, duck, quail, rabbit and goat.

Chicken with herbed feta crust

This dish was created by accident. I started to prepare a herbed feta dip for some friends, but for some reason changed my mind and decided to coat some chicken pieces with it instead, and bake them in the oven. It turned out to be one of the best chicken dishes I have ever prepared.

1–1.5 kg whole chicken,
    cleaned and spatchcocked
    or cut into pieces
sea salt and cracked pepper
extra virgin olive oil,
    for drizzling

Herbed feta crust
200 g Greek feta, cubed
2 small red chillies, seeded
    and chopped
¾ cup extra virgin olive oil
1 cup basil
3 tablespoons chopped
    spring onion
1 teaspoon dried wild oregano
1 tablespoon lemon juice
cracked pepper

Serves 4

Preheat the oven to 160°C and line a baking dish with baking paper.

Lay the chicken flat in the baking dish and season with a little salt and pepper.

Put all the ingredients for the herbed feta crust in a blender, and process until it forms a smooth mixture.

Pour the mixture over the chicken, making sure each section is well coated. Drizzle a little olive oil over the top and bake for 1–1½ hours until the top is cooked through. Serve with a green salad.

Lamb souvlakia

Lamb *souvlaki* is the king of all *souvlakia* and a great dish to add to your next barbecue. In Greece it is a popular fast food, eaten as is or wrapped in pita bread with some *tzatziki* (see page 39), salad and fried potatoes on the side. You can also make it with pork, chicken or vegetables. Or try one of my favourite variations, with swordfish (see page 119).

1 kg leg of lamb, deboned
   or lamb mini roast
sea salt and cracked pepper
1–2 teaspoons dried wild
   oregano
3 tablespoons extra virgin
   olive oil
1 red onion, cut into cubes
1 red capsicum (pepper),
   seeded and cut into chunks
2 lemons, cut into wedges
tzatziki (see page 39), to serve

Makes 10

Soak 10 wooden skewers in water for 1–2 hours to ensure they do not burn during cooking. Alternatively, use metal skewers.

Cut the lamb into 2 cm pieces and remove any excess fat. Place the pieces in a bowl and season with salt and pepper. Add the oregano and olive oil and mix well.

Thread a piece of lamb onto a skewer, then an onion segment, another piece of lamb, a chunk of capsicum, then another piece of lamb. Repeat to make 10 *souvlakia*.

Heat an oiled chargrill pan or barbecue, add the *souvlakia* and cook for about 5 minutes each side until cooked through and lightly browned. Remove to a plate, cover with foil and rest for 5 minutes. Serve with lemon wedges and *tzatziki*.

Hellenic filo pizza with lamb and tzatziki

Many believe that the idea of using bread as a plate came from the ancient Greeks, who ate flat round bread called *plankuntos*. The bread was baked with a variety of toppings and served as an accompaniment to braised dishes and soups. These days, Greek pizza is made with pita bread; however, I prefer to make it with a lighter, crunchier filo base. This is a brilliant recipe for using up leftover baked lamb.

1 tablespoon extra virgin olive
    oil, plus extra for brushing
2 red onions, thinly sliced
1 teaspoon honey
sea salt and cracked pepper
10 sheets filo pastry
250 g *haloumi*, grated
500 g baked lamb, thinly
    sliced
14 sundried tomatoes, drained
24 Kalamata olives, seeds
    removed
½ cup chopped mint
1 lemon
tzatziki (see page 39), to serve

Serves 4

Preheat the oven to 180°C.

Heat the olive oil in a frying pan over medium heat and cook the onion for about 5 minutes. Add the honey, salt and pepper and cook for 3–5 minutes until the onion is golden brown and softened. Remove the pan from the heat.

Brush a rectangular baking tin with olive oil. Place two pieces of filo in the base of the tin, allowing some to hang over the sides, and brush well with olive oil. Place another two sheets of filo on top and brush with olive oil (cover the remaining sheets of filo with a tea towel to prevent them drying out).

Sprinkle half the *haloumi* over the filo base, top with two more filo sheets and brush with olive oil. Finish layering the remaining filo sheets, brushing every second sheet with oil.

Sprinkle the remaining *haloumi* over the final layer of filo, followed by the caramelised onion, sundried tomatoes, olives, some of the chopped mint and a little cracked pepper.

Bake for 15 minutes. Add the pieces of lamb. Continue to bake for another 10–15 minutes until the filo is golden brown and crisp at the edges. Remove from the oven and squeeze lemon juice over the pizza. Cut into slices and top each piece with a teaspoon of *tzatziki*. Garnish the remaining chopped mint.

Mrs Poulopoulos (middle with scarf around her head) with friends and family, pictured in Hyde Park, Sydney, a couple of weeks after arriving, in 1957

Mrs Poulopolous with her husband and son, Antonios, in 1960

Mrs Poulopoulos's empty suitcase

Mrs Niki Poulopoulos is another friend of my aunt Stavroula's. Her passion for Greek food is so intoxicating that I believe she could turn anyone into a fan after just one sitting.

She was born and raised in Athens in an area near the city centre, called Moschato. In those days Athens was very different to what it is today. There were not as many buildings and there were many acres of land available, where people grazed their goats and grew their olives, fruit and vegetables, and other produce to ensure their survival. A well supplied Niki's family's water.

'We were poor but happy. We made do with what little we had and we loved one another,' she says. Mrs Poulopoulos lived with her mother, sister and brother in a small rented house; her father had passed away when she was 11 years old. Her mother worked at a flour mill, where she was responsible for sewing the sacks. Her sister was responsible for taking care of the family and ensuring all the household chores were completed. Niki attended school to learn how to sew.

Although life was difficult she recalls many happy moments. She remembers the Tuesday at Easter time when they would celebrate at the *platia*, or main square. They would dance, eat, drink and be merry. She also remembers the celebrations at *protomagia*, or May Day, 1 May each year. This was a celebration of spring and the day would be set aside for a country outing. The women would make the traditional Easter bread to take to each of their mothers-in-law.

When families in the area prepared their meals they would take their dishes and their bread to a communal oven to be cooked. The oven was quite a walk from Mrs Poulopoulos's house but it was her responsibility to take the food to be cooked. Everyone always knew what everyone else was cooking and would discuss the various dishes.

Mrs Poulopoulos married in Greece when she was 18 and came to Australia with her young son in 1957, at the age of 22. Her husband had arrived a year earlier. 'I came for a better life,' she says. She came with just one suitcase but she was still over the weight limit for luggage. The men at the airport emptied her suitcase without her knowledge and removed all her dresses, leaving her with only belts and shoes. She only discovered she had no clothes to wear when she arrived at her new home.

She recalls crying day and night for the first six months after she arrived in Australia and she couldn't bear to leave her home in Paddington, Sydney. She longed to be back in Greece. Her family urged her to find a job and to get out of the house. Instead, she would make sandwiches for her lunch and spend most of her day at the park opposite Saint Vincent's hospital. She would cry miserably and then return home at 3 p.m. Her family assumed she had been out looking for work all day. Eventually, however, she settled down a little and found work in a shirt factory on Oxford Street.

Mrs Poulopoulos reminisces often about her years in Greece. She misses family members who remained in Greece, as well as the culture. Many of the recipes that she enjoys cooking reconnect her with her homeland and they are all documented in her recipe book. She has learnt many recipes from her mother and also some from her friends here in Australia. 'I always cook your aunt's *galaktoboureko*,' she tells me (see recipe on page 144). She also particularly enjoys making traditional Greek dishes such as yoghurt cake (see recipe on page 196), pumpkin pie and *rolo*, a minced-meat roll with whole eggs in the middle (see recipe over the page).

Mrs Poulopoulos's rolo

Rolo is a Greek version of meatloaf, and Mrs Poulopoulos has given me her wonderful recipe for it. She recommends that you serve it with *poure* (mashed potato), French fries or rice pilaf.

1 kg minced beef or lamb,
    or a mixture of both
4 tablespoons dried
    breadcrumbs
2 eggs, lightly beaten
3 tablespoons chopped mint
3 tablespoons chopped
    flat-leaf parsley
3 tablespoons plain flour,
    plus extra for dusting
sea salt and cracked pepper
4 eggs, extra, hard-boiled
2–3 tablespoons extra virgin
    olive oil

Cherry tomato sauce
500 g cherry tomatoes
2 bay leaves
½ teaspoon ground cloves
½ teaspoon ground allspice
sea salt and cracked pepper

Serves 4

Place the minced meat, breadcrumbs, beaten egg, mint, parsley, flour, salt and pepper in a bowl and mix with your hands until well combined. Divide the mixture into two equal portions.

Spread out two large pieces of plastic wrap on a flat surface, place a portion of the meat mixture on each and form into an oval shape.

Remove the shell from the hard-boiled eggs and place two whole eggs in a row down the centre of each roll, pressing them gently into the meat. Lift the plastic wrap and use to roll the meat rolls, neatening the oval shape.

Sprinkle some flour on a plate, add the meat rolls and carefully roll them around until well coated in flour.

Heat the olive oil in a large saucepan over medium heat. Carefully add the meat rolls and pan-fry lightly on all sides until they are golden brown. Add the sauce ingredients, then reduce the heat to low and simmer, covered, for 30–45 minutes until the tomatoes have formed a sauce and the rolls are cooked through.

Wine-braised chicken livers with deep-fried basil pasta

My aunt Stavroula would regularly pan-fry chicken livers with olive oil, oregano, salt and pepper and then add lemon juice, before serving them on pasta with lots of grated cheese. This is my version. I wanted to add a bit more colour and texture so I have fried the pasta and basil to give a bit of crunch. If you do not have basil, you could use flat-leaf parsley instead.

300 g chicken livers
olive oil, for pan-frying
1 small red onion, chopped
sea salt and cracked pepper
1 teaspoon ground cinnamon
2 sprigs rosemary
4 sprigs thyme
½ cup red wine
125 g spaghetti
3 tablespoons whole
  basil leaves
grated *myzithra*, *kefalotiri*
  or *kefalograviera* cheese,
  to serve

Serves 4

Trim the chicken livers, cutting off any dark sections, then wash and drain on kitchen paper.

Heat about 2 tablespoons olive oil in a frying pan over medium heat and sauté the onion. Add the chicken livers and cook for about 2 minutes until browned on all sides. Season with salt and pepper, add the cinnamon, rosemary, thyme and wine and bring to a simmer. Reduce the heat to low and braise for 10–15 minutes until the wine has almost evaporated and the chicken livers are cooked and tender.

Meanwhile, bring a saucepan of salted water to the boil and cook the pasta according to the packet instructions. Drain well.

Pour enough olive oil into a frying pan to cover the base. Heat until very hot, then add the pasta and cook until the bottom is golden brown and crisp. (You could also use a deep-fryer for this.) Turn over and cook the other side. Drain on kitchen paper to absorb any excess oil.

In the same frying pan, heat a little more olive oil until quite hot. Add the basil leaves and cook for just a few seconds until they shrivel up and become crispy. Make sure you stand back when you do this as the oil can splatter quite a bit. Quickly remove the basil and drain on kitchen paper.

Arrange the pasta on a serving platter, sprinkle with the basil and place the chicken livers in the middle. Serve hot, topped with grated cheese.

Cinnamon-rubbed chicken stuffed with rice, pine nuts and grapes

This is very much a summer dish, and the stuffing capitalises on seasonal ingredients such as grapes. I always think of the Peloponnesian countryside when I make it, as grape vines seem to grow along the side of most of the roads there. I have used both red and green grapes because they give a vibrant colour to the dish, and the wine adds a bit of an edge.

1–1.5 kg whole chicken
sea salt and cracked pepper
2 teaspoons ground cinnamon
4 tablespoons extra virgin
  olive oil
750 g seedless white grapes
500 g seedless red grapes
6 spring onions, chopped
½ cup rice, preferably a blend
  that includes some wild rice
½ cup chopped flat-leaf
  parsley
½ cup chopped mint
1¼ cups sweet white wine
50 g pine nuts, toasted

Serves 4

Clean the chicken well, remove the insides and pat dry. Combine some salt and pepper, 1 teaspoon of the cinnamon and 3 tablespoons of the olive oil and use to coat the chicken inside and out. Place in a baking dish.

Wash the grapes and remove them from the stem. Juice some of the green grapes to make about 1 cup of grape juice.

Preheat the oven to 180°C.

Heat the remaining olive oil in a skillet or frying pan over moderate heat and cook the spring onion, rice, parsley and mint for 1–2 minutes. Add ¾ cup of the wine, pine nuts, grapes and remaining cinnamon and season with salt and pepper. Stir well to combine, then reduce the heat to low and simmer until the wine has evaporated.

Remove from the heat and let the mixture cool for about 10 minutes, then spoon it into the cavity of the chicken.

Pour the grape juice and remaining white wine around the chicken, cover the baking dish with foil and bake for 30 minutes. Reduce the temperature to 160°C, remove the foil and bake for a further hour until the chicken is golden brown and cooked through.

Place the chicken on a platter and cut it in half to reveal the wonderful stuffing. Pour some of the juices from the baking dish over the top and serve hot with salad and baked potatoes (see page 107).

Moussaka

This has got to be the classic Greek dish, but there is still room to make the recipe your own. For instance, I sometimes grate Greek cheeses such as *kefalograviera*, *kefalotiri* or *myzithra* and mix this through the béchamel sauce. To eliminate unwelcome lumps in the sauce, I use either a non-stick saucepan and a wooden spoon, or a stainless steel saucepan with a whisk.

1 kg minced lean beef or
    lamb, or a combination
    of both
1 large white onion, finely
    chopped
2 cloves garlic, thinly sliced
sea salt and cracked pepper
1–2 teaspoons ground
    nutmeg, plus extra
    to garnish
1 teaspoon ground cloves
1 teaspoon ground cinnamon
2–3 tablespoons tomato paste
extra virgin olive oil,
    for brushing
2 large eggplants (aubergines),
    cut into 1 cm thick slices
5 zucchini (courgettes), sliced
2 tablespoons extra virgin
    olive oil, extra
5 potatoes, sliced

Béchamel sauce
50 g unsalted butter
5 tablespoons flour
1.5 litres milk
2 egg yolks

Serves 8

Place the minced meat, onion, garlic, salt, pepper and spices in a saucepan over medium heat and cook, stirring constantly, until the meat browns. It is important that you keep mixing to break up any clumps of meat – it must be smooth. Add the tomato paste and cook for 5 minutes over low heat. Set aside for at least 30 minutes to cool to room temperature.

Preheat the oven to 180°C.

Meanwhile, heat a lightly oiled chargrill pan over medium heat. Brush the eggplant and zucchini slices with olive oil on both sides and cook for about 4 minutes each side until golden brown. Drain on a platter lined with kitchen paper.

Heat the extra olive oil in a frying pan and cook the potato slices until they are golden brown. Drain on a platter lined with kitchen paper.

Line the base of a very long and deep baking dish with potatoes. Discard any excess liquid from the meat mixture, then spoon about half of it over the potatoes. Next, have a layer of eggplant, followed by the remaining meat mixture. Finish with a layer of zucchini slices.

To make the béchamel sauce, place the flour and butter in a saucepan over low heat and stir constantly until the butter has melted and the flour has been absorbed to form a paste (or *roux*). Gradually add small amounts of milk, stirring constantly until the milk is absorbed before adding the next batch – don't rush this stage or the sauce will be lumpy. Continue until all the milk has been added and you have a thick, smooth sauce. Remove the pan from the heat before the sauce starts to bubble, add the egg yolks and mix well.

Pour the sauce over the zucchini layer and sprinkle a little extra nutmeg over the top. Bake for 1–1¼ hours until cooked through and golden brown. Leave to stand for 15 minutes before serving.

Pastitsio

This version of *pastitsio* is one of my favourite dishes and I make it whenever I have something to celebrate. I just love the combination of the pasta, minced meat and béchamel sauce. The secret is to coat the pasta with egg whites and cheese – this ensures the cut portions will stay together when the dish is served. If you can't find *kefalotiri* or *kefalograviera* cheese, use any other salty grating cheese instead.

2 tablespoons extra virgin
    olive oil
1 kg minced lean beef
2 white onions, finely
    chopped
2 cloves garlic, finely chopped
1 whole nutmeg
1 tablespoon ground nutmeg,
    plus extra to garnish
sea salt and cracked pepper
2 large tomatoes, chopped
1 cup chopped flat-leaf parsley
750 g penne pasta
2 egg whites
1 cup grated *kefalotiri* or
    kefalograviera cheese
1 tablespoon chopped basil

Béchamel sauce
5 tablespoons flour
50 g unsalted butter
1.5 litres milk
2 egg yolks

Serves 4–6

Heat the olive oil in a large saucepan over medium heat, add the minced meat, onion, garlic, whole and ground nutmeg, salt and pepper and stir constantly until the meat browns. It is important that you keep mixing to break up any clumps of meat. Reduce the heat to low, add the tomato and parsley and cook for about 2 minutes. Set aside to cool for at least 30 minutes.

Preheat the oven to 180°C.

Cook the pasta in in a saucepan of salted boiling water until slightly undercooked (it will cook further in the oven). Drain and place in a bowl. Beat the egg whites until frothy and mix through the pasta. Drain the pasta again to remove any excess egg white, then return to the bowl and add the grated cheese.

Place a thick layer of pasta in a large, deep baking dish so the base is completely covered. Spoon the minced meat mixture on top. Arrange the rest of the pasta on top of the meat so it is completely covered.

To make the béchamel sauce, place the flour and butter in a saucepan over low heat and stir constantly until the butter has melted and the flour has been absorbed to form a paste (or *roux*). Gradually add small amounts of milk, stirring constantly until the milk is absorbed before adding the next batch – don't rush this stage or the sauce will be lumpy. Continue until all the milk has been added and you have a thick, smooth sauce. Remove the pan from the heat before the sauce starts to bubble, add the egg yolks and mix well.

Pour the béchamel over the pasta, sprinkle with a little ground nutmeg and bake for about 1 hour until the top is golden brown. Leave to stand for 15–20 minutes before serving. Garnish with basil just before taking the dish to the table. Serve hot or at room temperature.

Moussaka and *pastitsio*

Gemista

The Greeks have been stuffing anything and everything for hundreds of years, a tradition that continues to this day. *Gemista* are vegetables filled with rice, meats, seafood or vegetables. In this version, I have stuffed ripe tomatoes with a minced beef and rice filling, but you could also use eggplant, capsicum or vine leaves, and the fresh herbs and zucchini are optional in the filling. Serve the tomatoes hot or cold.

10 medium tomatoes
3 tablespoons finely chopped
    flat-leaf parsley
3 tablespoons finely
    chopped dill
4 tablespoons pine nuts
2 zucchini (courgettes), grated
3 tablespoons extra virgin
    olive oil, plus extra for
    drizzling
8 spring onions, finely
    chopped
500 g minced lean beef
2 teaspoons ground cinnamon
4 tablespoons short-grain rice
sea salt and cracked pepper
tzatziki (see page 39) or
    Greek-style yoghurt,
    to serve

Makes 10

Preheat the oven to 180°C.

Cut the tops off the tomatoes and set aside for later use. Hollow out the tomatoes by removing all the seeds and flesh with a spoon or melon baller. Place the pulp in a bowl and add the parsley, dill, pine nuts and zucchini.

Heat the olive oil in a frying pan or skillet over low heat and cook the spring onion for 5 minutes or until softened. Add the minced beef and sauté for about 5 minutes until browned. Stir in the cinnamon and rice and season with salt and pepper. Remove the pan from the heat and let the mixture cool slightly.

Add the beef mixture to the tomato mixture and season to taste. Mix until well combined, then spoon the filling into the tomatoes and put the tomato 'lids' back on.

Place the filled tomatoes in a baking dish and drizzle a little extra virgin olive oil over the top. Season with salt and pepper. Pour some water into the base of the baking dish to a depth of about 5 mm.

Place the dish in the oven and bake for about 1 hour until cooked through. Turn off the oven and let the tomatoes sit in the oven for half an hour before serving. Remove carefully from the baking dish, using two spoons so that no stuffing escapes. Serve with *tzatziki* or Greek-style yoghurt.

Chicken avgolemono soup

Soupa is nourishment for body and soul, and this is the dish I always take to friends who have the flu or are otherwise unwell. You are guaranteed to recover after a dose of it! *Avgolemono* means 'egg and lemon' in Greek. In this version, I have used chicken, but alternatively you could use snapper, goat or lamb. My aunt Stavroula would often make it with a whole snapper and add carrots, celery, onions and potatoes.

1–1.5 kg whole chicken
 (or you could use various
 chicken cuts)
8–10 cups water, depending
 on the size of your pan
½ bunch parsley, tied
4 sprigs thyme
2 sticks celery, halved
2 carrots, halved
4 onions, halved
¾ cup short-grain white rice
4 eggs, separated
1 cup lemon juice
cracked pepper or lemon
 pepper

Serves 4–6

Clean the chicken well and remove the insides. Pat dry and cut into pieces.

Place the chicken pieces in a large saucepan and pour in enough water to cover. Bring to the boil over low heat, skimming any scum off the surface. Add the parsley, thyme, celery, carrot and onion and simmer gently for 45 minutes until the chicken is tender and cooked through.

Transfer the chicken pieces to a plate. When cool enough to handle, remove the chicken meat from the bones and take off the skin. Cut the meat into small pieces.

Chop the celery, carrot and onion and return them to the stock, along with the chicken pieces. Discard the parsley and thyme.

Bring the stock to a simmer, add the rice and cook, stirring, for 5–10 minutes until the rice is almost cooked. Meanwhile, beat the egg whites in a large bowl until frothy. Add the egg yolks, then gradually add the lemon juice, beating constantly. Continue beating while slowly adding some of the hot stock until the bowl is almost full. Pour the *avgolemono* mixture into the pan of remaining stock and mix well. Simmer over low heat for a further 5 minutes.

Garnish with a little pepper and serve with crusty bread.

Mrs Michaelides's smoked Cypriot sausage

This sausage (*loukanika*) is seasoned with coriander, soaked in red wine and smoked. The traditional cooking method (given below) takes some time, but if you're pressed for time or don't have a smoker, a quick alternative is to combine all the ingredients except the casing and roll the mixture into small sausage shapes or balls. Fry them in olive oil and squeeze some lemon juice on top just before serving.

Skinos is a berry similar to a juniper berry. Some Greeks have a *skinos* tree in their backyard. Juniper berries are a good substitute.

3 kg minced pork
sea salt and cracked pepper
3 tablespoons coriander seeds, crushed
2 litres dry red wine, such as claret
3 tablespoons *skinos* or juniper berries, toasted and crushed
sausage casings (ask your butcher for these)

Serves 12

Combine the minced pork, salt, pepper and coriander in a bowl and refrigerate overnight.

Warm the wine in a saucepan, then remove from the heat and cool to room temperature. Mix the wine through the meat, then add the *skinos* and a little more salt and pepper. Cover and marinate in the fridge for 8 days.

Clean the sausage casings and stuff with the pork mixture. Prick each sausage once so the excess wine runs out.

Heat up a smoker and place the sausages inside. Use a mild wood and smoke at a low temperature of about 160°C so the sausages take on a lovely flavour. Remove after 6 or 7 hours, before they start to shrink and dry out. Serve as an appetiser or as part of a *meze* plate.

Mrs Michaelides's endratha

In other regions of Greece this dish is known as fricassée. Fricassée is a method of cooking whereby meat or poultry is slowly braised with vegetables or herbs and then finished off with *avgolemono* (egg and lemon sauce). The *avgolemono* counteracts the richness of the lamb and makes a tangy, creamy sauce. The region Mrs Michaelides comes from makes this dish with potatoes and parsley (see the 'vine leaf lady's' story on pages 58–9).

4 tablespoons olive oil
500 g lamb shanks
1 onion, chopped
1 cup water
2 tablespoons chopped
    flat-leaf parsley
sea salt and cracked pepper
4 potatoes, cut into thick
    wedges
2 tablespoons plain flour,
    dissolved in ½ cup water
2 eggs, separated
3 tablespoons lemon juice
ground cinnamon, to garnish

Serves 4

Heat the olive oil in a deep frying pan or large saucepan and brown the lamb shanks on all sides. Add the onion and cook until soft and brown. Stir in the water, parsley, salt and pepper and simmer, covered, over low heat for about 15–20 minutes.

About 10 minutes into the cooking process, add the potatoes. When the potatoes are cooked, add the dissolved flour and stir well to combine. Remove the pan from the heat and leave to cool.

Beat the egg whites in a large bowl until frothy, then beat in the egg yolks. Continue beating while slowly adding some of the hot stock to the bowl. Pour the *avgolemono* mixture into the pan, shake the pan well, then return to the heat and simmer gently for 2–3 minutes so the egg can cook.

Transfer to a serving dish and sprinkle with ground cinnamon. Serve with fresh bread to mop up the juices.

Traditional Greek lamb with pasta

For this recipe I use *kritharaki* (a Greek version of risoni), but you could use any other small pasta. I usually make this is in a *youvetsi* (clay baking dish) just like they do in Greece, as I find food more flavoursome when it's cooked this way, but if you don't have one use a regular baking dish instead.

1–1.5 kg leg of lamb,
   cleaned and some of
   the fat trimmed off
6 cloves garlic, peeled
12 cloves
12 whole black peppercorns
sea salt and cracked pepper
1 teaspoon dried wild oregano
extra virgin olive oil, for
   drizzling
1–2 cups warm water
200 g *kritharaki* pasta
2 large tomatoes, chopped or
   400 g tin chopped tomatoes
grated *myzithra*, *kefalotiri* or
   kefalograviera cheese,
   to garnish (optional)
chopped flat-leaf parsley,
   to garnish (optional)

Serves 4–6

Preheat the oven to 180°C.

Cut six incisions in the lamb and fill each one with a clove of garlic, two cloves and two peppercorns. Rub the lamb all over with salt, pepper and oregano and drizzle with plenty of olive oil.

Place the lamb in a *youvetsi* or baking dish and add 1 cup of warm water. Cover with foil and bake for 1 hour.

About 10 minutes before the end of this cooking time, place the *kritharaki* in a pan of salted boiling water and cook for 8 minutes or until almost cooked. Drain.

Remove the lamb from the oven and place the *kritharaki* around it. Spoon the tomato over the *kritharaki* and season with salt and pepper. Return to the oven and bake, uncovered, for a further 30 minutes until the lamb is cooked and coming off the bone. Check the water level occasionally and add more water when the first cup has evaporated. Remove from the oven and leave to rest for 15 minutes before serving.

To serve, sprinkle some grated *myzithra* or one of the other cheeses over the *kritharaki* and a little over the lamb, followed by chopped parsley (if using).

Mrs Gouma's Christmas turkey with Constantinople-style stuffing

In our family we cook turkey just once a year – at Christmas. In the Greek Orthodox calendar, Christmas is an extremely important festive and spiritual occasion, a time to reflect and spend loving moments with family. This recipe was passed on to my aunt Stavroula by two special family friends, Mr and Mrs Gouma. It has been in their family since the Byzantine period and originates from Constantinople. We usually prepare the turkey the night before Christmas and place it in the oven around 10 p.m., taking it out at lunchtime the next day. This slow cooking results in soft, tender and juicy meat.

5 tablespoons extra virgin
   olive oil
2 large white onions, chopped
sea salt and cracked pepper
1.5 kg minced beef
2 whole nutmegs
7 kg whole turkey
1½ cups pine nuts
1 cup dried breadcrumbs
1 cup sultanas
½ cup olive oil
½ cup lemon juice

Serves 10–12

Heat the olive oil in a saucepan, add the onion, salt, pepper and minced meat and cook, stirring constantly, until the meat browns. It is important that you keep mixing to break up any clumps of meat

Add the nutmegs and cook over low heat for 1 hour. Remove from the heat and leave to cool to room temperature.

In the meantime, clean the turkey and pat dry. Place in a very large baking dish and refrigerate until the meat mixture is ready.

Preheat the oven to 140°C.

Add the pine nuts, breadcrumbs and sultanas to the cooled meat mixture and mix well. Place the stuffing in all the cavities of the turkey, including the neck, then sew up (using a needle and thread) to secure the stuffing. Season the turkey with salt and pepper, then pour on the olive oil and lemon juice.

Cover with foil and bake overnight for 12 hours. In the morning, a few hours before the end of the cooking time, remove the foil so that the turkey can brown on top. Baste the turkey every so often. This is best served simply with fresh salad.

Rabbit stifado with saffron mash

A *stifado* is the Greek way of braising or stewing meat in red wine and red wine vinegar. For this recipe I have chosen rabbit – which is a lovely meat, but does need to marinate overnight to balance out its strong flavour. The saffron gives the mash a lovely colour and an unusual flavour. You'll need to start this recipe the day before.

1–1.5 kg rabbit, cut into
  pieces
½ cup extra virgin olive oil
12 pickling onions, peeled
6 sprigs thyme, tied in a
  bunch
1 tablespoon ground allspice
sea salt and cracked pepper
1 teaspoon sugar
1 cinnamon stick
2 bay leaves
2 cups red wine
2 large tomatoes, chopped

Marinade
1½ cups dry red wine
3 bay leaves
8 whole allspice berries
1 cinnamon stick

Saffron mash
1 kg potatoes, peeled
½ cup fresh cream
½–1 level teaspoon
  saffron threads
20 g butter

Serves 4

Wash the rabbit and pat dry with kitchen paper.

Combine all the marinade ingredients in a bowl. Add the rabbit, then cover and marinate in the refrigerator overnight, turning the rabbit occasionally.

Heat 3 tablespoons olive oil in a large heavy-based saucepan over medium heat and cook the onions for about 5 minutes until they are browned. Shake the pan around while the onions are cooking. Remove and place in a bowl.

Remove the rabbit from the marinade and pat dry. Heat the remaining olive oil in the pan and sear the rabbit pieces over medium–high heat until they are brown on both sides. Add the thyme, allspice, salt, pepper, sugar, cinnamon stick and bay leaves, then pour in the wine and tomatoes. Reduce the heat and simmer, covered, for 1½–2 hours until the rabbit is tender.

When the rabbit is nearly ready, begin making the mash. Place the potatoes in a saucepan of salted water and boil for 15–20 minutes until soft.

Meanwhile, pour the cream into a separate saucepan and warm gently over very low heat. Remove from the heat as soon as the cream is warm, add the saffron threads and leave to infuse for a few minutes.

Drain the potatoes and return to the pan. Place over low heat, add the butter to the potatoes and mash them. Add the cream slowly to the potato, mashing and mixing constantly until smooth and creamy. Serve with the rabbit *stifado*.

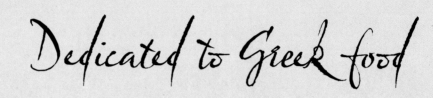

Dedicated to Greek food

In August 2004, I went on a life-changing trip to Greece. It was my first visit back there since leaving Psara all those years before.

While there, I visited Kalamata and many of the beautiful islands. However, it was on the island of Mykonos that my life changed forever, when I visited the small church of Saint Fanourios. It was there that my decision to pursue my passion for food was sealed and my destiny set on a new course.

Saint Fanourios is a very small church on one of the main winding streets in Mykonos. Beautifully whitewashed, the Greek flag hangs proudly outside. It had an inviting look about it and I felt compelled to go in and light a candle. The church was adorned with beautiful icons painted with vibrant colours and finished off with gold and silver. In the corner there were many candles that had being lit that day by people who had passed by. I felt a peace in my soul that I had not experienced before and the sweet fragrance of the holy basil heightened my sense of tranquillity.

Suddenly I experienced an epiphany and saw all that was about to happen in my life pass before me. I realised it was time for me to re-invent my life, and in that church I saw a new path set out for me to follow. I decided there and then that I was going to dedicate myself to bringing Greek food and culture to my fellow Australians and to the rest of the world.

I can only describe the experience as Henry Miller did in *The Colossus of Maroussi*, when he wrote:

> *Everything here speaks now, as it did centuries ago, of illumination.*
> *Here the light penetrates directly to the soul, opens the door and*

windows of the heart, makes one naked, exposed, isolated in a
metaphysical bliss which makes everything clear without being known.

I was aware when I came out of the church that a very important
decision had been made in my heart and soul, and I felt empowered
and inspired. I could not wait to embark on my new adventure in food.

Outside the church was an old man, and I greeted him in Greek. He
looked at me intently and then stated that it seemed that I had found
what I was looking for. I was surprised to hear his words and asked
why he had said this.

He proceeded to explain that the church was named after Saint
Fanourios, the patron saint of lost things. People invoke his name in
prayers whenever they want to recover lost items or be reunited with
lost loved ones. He is commemorated on 27 August, the day the icon
of him displayed in the church was found. I was fascinated by what
the old man told me and interested to hear more.

He shared many stories with me, about people who had found good
health or located lost loved ones. These touching and beautiful stories
were like fairytales out of a book. I was there for what seemed like
hours, discussing my future plans and my life with this complete
stranger. When we parted he gave me a small icon of Saint Fanourios
and wished me well.

I will always remember that day. I have since returned to Greece several
times and of course I visit Saint Fanourios each time. He has found a
special place in my heart and life. I keep the icon of Saint Fanourios
on my fridge, to bless my kitchen and all the friends and family whom
I welcome into my home.

Sweets and other special things

Greek people have something to celebrate almost every day of the year. There are birthdays, weddings, christenings and countless religious celebrations. Even if there isn't an official reason to party, we Greeks will think of something! Savoury dishes are a big part of the festive table, naturally, but perhaps more important are the various sweets: *kourambiethes*, *baklava* and *vasilopita*, as well as many other delights. Every mouthful salutes the flavours of Greece, from the nuts, honey, yoghurt, cinnamon and *masticha* to spiced wine and strong sweet coffee. I like to think this is how the ancient Greek gods themselves would have celebrated.

Spoon sweets

A 'spoon sweet' is a traditional offering made to a visitor, literally a sweet welcome to the friendly environment of a Greek home. They are called spoon sweets because the usual serving size is a well-filled teaspoon, and they are accompanied by a cup of strong Greek coffee and a glass of icy cold water.

Most of these sweets are prepared when a particular fruit is in season, preserved for the days when it is not available. They can be made with cherries, grapes, figs, apricots, berries, olives and watermelon; citrus fruit such as bitter wild orange and cumquat from Corfu; capers and tomatoes from Santorini; and nuts such as pistachios and walnuts. The most unusual spoon sweets are those made with rose petals or other types of flower petals, masticha and eggplant. It is traditional to add a couple of geranium leaves to spoon sweets, which adds to both the fragrance and the flavour.

I love to serve spoon sweets over ice-cream or Greek-style yoghurt spiked with lots of cinnamon. Here are a few of my favourite recipes.

Cherry spoon sweet

I love cherries and find it disappointing that they're not in season during winter. I get around this problem by making large jars of this spoon sweet.

1 kg cherries, washed
¾ cup castor sugar
1 cup water
1 cinnamon stick
4 cloves
3 tablespoons lemon juice
a few geranium leaves
  (optional)

Fills a 500 g jar

Remove the cherry stones using a cherry pitter. Place in a heavy-based saucepan and add the sugar, water, cinnamon and cloves. Bring to the boil over medium heat, then add the lemon juice and simmer over low heat for about 30 minutes until thickened, skimming any foam off the top. The mixture is ready when it bubbles and starts to caramelise.

Remove the pan from the heat and set aside to cool. Pour the syrup into a sterilised jar and seal. Serve with a few geranium leaves, if using.

From left to right:
Grape spoon sweet with slivered
almonds, lemon zest spoon sweet
and cherry spoon sweet

Halva with cherry spoon sweet >

This sweet is very popular in Greece during Lent and other fasts. It is incredibly easy to prepare and I usually make it when I have friends coming over. You can use baking tins or moulds in whatever shape you like – try this with other spoon sweets too.

2½ cups water
¾ cup castor sugar
½ cup semolina
½ cup toasted, slivered
  almonds
½ cup raisins
½ teaspoon ground cinnamon
dash of rosewater
olive oil, for brushing
12 teaspoons cherry spoon
  sweet (see page 180)
Greek-style yoghurt, to serve
honey, to serve

Makes 8

Combine the water and sugar in a saucepan and stir over medium heat until the sugar has dissolved. Add the semolina a little at a time, stirring until the mixture thickens. Remove the pan from the heat as soon as the mixture starts to boil and stir in the almonds, raisins, cinnamon and rosewater.

Brush a 12-mould muffin tray with olive oil. Pour the mixture in the moulds, then place in the fridge for 2 hours or until set.

Turn the moulds out onto each plate and place a teaspoon of cherry spoon sweet on top of each one. Serve with a dollop of honeyed yoghurt.

Lemon zest spoon sweet

400 g thinly sliced lemon
  zest (peeled off fresh,
  clean lemons)
½ cup castor sugar
1 tablespoon honey
¾ cup water
1 cinnamon stick
4 cloves
1 tablespoon lemon juice

Fills a 250 g jar

Combine the lemon zest, sugar, honey, water, cinnamon stick and cloves in a heavy-based saucepan. Bring to the boil over medium heat, then add the lemon juice and simmer over low heat for about 30 minutes until thickened, skimming any foam off the top. The mixture is ready when it bubbles and starts to caramelise.

Remove the pan from the heat and set aside to cool. Pour the syrup into a sterilised jar and seal.

My Aunt Stavroula's quince
spoon sweet and grape spoon
sweet with slivered almonds

< My Aunt Stavroula's quince spoon sweet

I love to make jars of this when quince is in season and serve it as a spoon sweet to accompany a cheese platter, or simply add it to yoghurt or ice-cream.

1 kg quince
900 g castor sugar
2¼ cups water
1 cinnamon stick
7 cloves
juice of 1 lemon

Fills a 750 g jar

Clean the quince, remove the cores and cut into thin slices.

Combine the quince, sugar, water, cinnamon stick and cloves in a heavy-based saucepan. Bring to the boil over medium heat, then simmer over low heat until thick and syrupy, skimming any foam off the top. Towards the end of the cooking process, add the lemon juice.

Remove the pan from the heat and set aside to cool. Pour the syrup into a sterilised jar and seal.

< Grape spoon sweet with slivered almonds

It is important to use white seedless grapes for this recipe – the skin of red grapes separates from the flesh, leaving an unpleasant texture in the mouth. I have added toasted almonds to add a bit of crunch and a wonderful flavour.

1 kg white seedless grapes
3 cups castor sugar
3 tablespoons water
1 cinnamon stick
4 cloves
juice of 1 lemon
100 g slivered almonds,
    toasted

Fills a 750 g jar

Wash the grapes well and remove them from the stem.

Place the grapes in a heavy-based saucepan, add the sugar, water, cinnamon and cloves and bring to the boil over high heat. When the mixture begins to boil, reduce the heat to medium and simmer for about 45 minutes until thickened, skimming any foam off the top. Stir in the lemon juice and simmer for a further 15 minutes. The mixture is ready when it bubbles and starts to caramelise.

Remove the pan from the heat and stir in the almonds. Set aside to cool. Pour the syrup into a sterilised jar and seal.

Loukoumades >

This is my family's recipe for *loukoumades* – Greek-style doughnuts. They are best eaten warm, so if you have any left over, reheat them in the oven before serving. In the wintertime you can replace the walnuts with chopped toasted chestnuts.

1 teaspoon dried yeast
1 cup warm water
2 cups plain flour
1 teaspoon sea salt
1¼ cups cold water
olive oil, for deep-frying
honey, to serve
ground cinnamon, to garnish
½ cup walnuts, finely chopped

Makes about 30

Dissolve the yeast in the warm water.

Place the flour and salt in a bowl and stir in the yeast mixture. Add 1 cup cold water and mix until you have a smooth thin paste (you may need to add an extra ¼ cup cold water). Cover and set aside for up to an hour until it rises and forms bubbles under the surface.

Pour olive oil into a deep frying pan to a depth of 4–5 cm and heat. Using a tablespoon, drop in large dollops of the mixture, one spoonful at a time. The mixture will form round dumplings. Fry for 2–3 minutes each side until golden brown, then remove and drain on kitchen paper. While still hot, pour some honey over the top and sprinkle with cinnamon and walnuts.

Roast chestnuts

Every time I eat chestnuts I think of the winter months in Greece where on most street corners you'll find someone selling fresh roast chestnuts in paper bags.

The prefecture of Karditsa, located in the middle of the Greek mainland, claims to have the largest chestnut production in Greece. Every October it celebrates with the annual Chestnut Festival.

1 kg fresh chestnuts

Serves 4

Preheat the oven to 180°C.

Put each chestnut on its side and cut halfway around the outer shell. I usually cut a cross. Spread the chestnuts out on a baking tray and roast for 25–30 minutes, turning them occasionally.

Serve while still warm. To eat, peel away the skin to expose the sweet white kernel.

My Aunt Stavroula's kourambiethes

Kourambiethes are traditional Greek almond shortbread cookies that we make for Easter and Christmas, and sometimes for other special occasions too. This is a recipe that my aunt has passed down to me.

½ cup blanched almonds
250 g unsalted butter,
    at room temperature
½ cup castor sugar
2 egg yolks
3 tablespoons *ouzo*
3 cups self-raising flour,
    sifted
½ teaspoon baking
    powder, sifted
½ cup icing sugar

Makes about 40

Preheat the oven to 140°C.

Thinly slice the almonds, place on a baking tray and toast in the oven for 5–10 minutes until lightly golden, stirring occasionally.

Increase the oven temperature to 160°C and line two baking trays with baking paper.

Place the butter and sugar in a bowl and beat at high speed using an electric mixer until pale and creamy. Add the egg yolks and *ouzo* and continue to mix.

Using a wooden spoon, slowly stir in the flour until the mixture is soft but not sticky. Add the baking powder and a little extra flour if necessary, and mix well.

Take 2 generous teaspoons of the mixture and knead it well for a minute or so. Flatten it out slightly and shape it into a round, or use pastry cutters to form other shapes, such as a Christmas tree. Repeat with the remaining dough.

Place on the baking trays, leaving a little space between them, and bake for about 25 minutes. The cookies are ready when they are crispy and very light golden brown. Transfer to a wire rack to cool.

Arrange the cooled cookies on a plate and sift generous amounts of icing sugar over the top before serving.

My Aunt Stavroula's vasilopita

This is the traditional cake served on New Year's Day. *Vasilopita* is prepared in memory of an act of charity made by Saint Basil to the poor people of his parish. He asked the wealthier members of his parish to make cakes with coins baked into them – slices were given to the poor, and those who found the coin within their piece were considered especially blessed for the year.

When the cake is cut, it is distributed according to tradition. The first piece is for Saint Basil, the second slice is for the house, the next for the most senior resident of the house and so on, down to the youngest child. Pieces are also cut for absent members of the household. Some families will cut a slice for the poor and even one for their farm animals. Of course, the tradition remains that whoever finds the coin will be blessed for the New Year.

1 heaped tablespoon *masticha*
500 g unsalted butter, at room temperature
3 cups castor sugar
12 eggs
1 cup fresh orange juice
grated zest of 2 oranges
1 heaped tablespoon ground cinnamon
3 teaspoons baking powder, sifted
6 cups self-raising flour, sifted
1 gold coin, wrapped in foil
¾ cup whole blanched almonds

Serves 10–12

Preheat the oven to 160°C and grease a large round cake tin.

If you have whole clusters of *masticha*, place them in a mortar with a little bit of sugar or flour and grind to a powder with the pestle.

Place the butter and sugar in an electric mixer and mix until pale and smooth. Add the eggs while still mixing, then add the *masticha*, orange juice and zest, cinnamon and baking powder and continue to mix. Finally, add the flour a little at a time until a thick but not dry dough is formed.

Turn out the dough into the cake tin and insert the gold coin. Use the almonds to write the number for the New Year on top. Bake for 1–1¼ hours until golden brown and the sides come away from the tin. A skewer inserted into the centre should come out clean. Cool to room temperature before serving.

< Fanouropita

Every August on Saint Fanourios' name day, I light the *kantili* (a vigil oil candle) and then proceed to make *Fanouropita* in his honour. It is extremely easy to make and is delicious on its own or with fresh cream whipped with a touch of cinnamon, served with a Greek coffee. The following recipe is my aunt's.

1 cup olive oil
1¼ cups fresh orange juice
2 teaspoons ground cinnamon
1 cup sugar
3 cups self-raising flour, sifted
1 cup walnuts, finely chopped
1 teaspoon baking powder, sifted

Serves 4–6

Preheat the oven to 160°C and line a 20–25 cm round cake tin with baking paper.

Place the olive oil, orange juice, cinnamon and sugar in a bowl and mix well with a wooden spoon until the sugar dissolves a little.

Gradually add the flour, mixing well, then add the walnuts, followed by the baking powder. Stir until well combined.

Pour the cake mix into the tin and bake for 15 minutes. Reduce the temperature to 130°C and bake for a further 40 minutes or until cooked (a skewer inserted into the centre should come out clean). Transfer to a wire rack to cool slightly. Serve warm or at room temperature.

Hippocrates' spiced wine

This is a great way to transform a plain bottle of red wine into something magical, and is also a good way to warm up during winter. The wine was originally strained through a *Hippocras* bag, named after the Greek physician Hippocrates. It is believed that he used this spiced wine to cure digestive problems as well as improve general health. Ideally it should be enjoyed as a digestive after a meal.

750 ml bottle red wine,
  such as merlot
4 tablespoons fresh
  orange juice
3 tablespoons honey
1 cinnamon stick
4 whole cloves
4 allspice berries
2 × 2 cm slices ginger

Makes about 3 cups

Combine all the ingredients in a saucepan and simmer over low heat for about 15 minutes. Strain the ingredients into a jug and serve hot. You can refrigerate any leftover wine and drink it chilled with a sprig of mint thrown in.

Family mealtimes

My family in Sydney always looked forward to our mealtime gatherings. Our dinner table every night would be adorned with many traditional Greek dishes. And there was always dessert to follow. Dishes would be placed on a hand-embroidered linen tablecloth to heighten the experience. Each and every tablecloth had a tale to tell. 'This is the one that your grandmother and I sewed. This little flower here was sewn by your mother,' my aunt Stavroula would inform me.

Each plate would be paired with the appropriate cutlery for each course and a white napkin placed underneath the forks. The silver cutlery and Royal Doulton plates with the gold edging were reserved for special occasions. 'Don't forget the bread,' my aunt would call out to me.

Our home in Coogee had a permanently fixed fragrance of Greek cuisine. Preparations for dinner would start in the morning and I would always wake up to the aroma of some Greek ingredient or other. It might be as simple as the smell of the morning coffee or the *gemista* (see page 166) – you could smell the sweet capsicums, tomatoes and eggplants slow-cooking in the oven. Perhaps it would be the garlic from my aunt's *tzatziki* (see page 39). We had two large fridges in our home and our kitchen cupboards were always stocked to the brim. There were always wonderful ingredients with which to whip up something for that unexpected guest.

My family encompassed my aunt Stavroula, my uncle George, my sister Katina, and my cousins, Manny, Chris and Con. Everyone in the family had their favourite dishes and my aunt would find a way to incorporate at least one person's favourite dish into the weekly menu. We would all quickly assemble at the dining-room table, which was strategically positioned next to the kitchen, as soon as my aunt called us. Each of us had our set position. My aunt sat on my left and my uncle on my right. My aunt was always the last to be seated, as there was always something to fuss over in the kitchen. We would wait for her to be seated for what seemed to me to be an agonisingly long time. Meanwhile, we would all show great restraint as we looked at all the fine food. My aunt would create magical dishes and I always felt very proud when I had assisted with their preparation.

Once my aunt was seated, a quick prayer would follow and the conversation would flow as each plate was filled to overflowing. My uncle would enlighten us with a story he had read that day in one of the Greek newspapers. What would be the topic today? Greek history, politics, religion or the merits of vitamin C? Although he had never had a formal education, my uncle loved to read and share his knowledge. He had an answer for everything. I dared not challenge him.

We all ate at different paces. My uncle and I were always the first to finish our meal for fear our full plate might be taken away. We would then leap on each dish as if we were starved animals and help ourselves to seconds. The conversation would flow on to the day's events and conclude with a judgement of the food. 'Was there too much salt? Perhaps I should've put in less *kefalotiri* cheese?' my aunt would ask. But the dishes always seemed perfect to us.

When we had all finished our meal my sister and I would quickly gather all the plates and wash up. We needed to hurry so that we could get to dessert. After tucking into a helping or two of dessert we would settle in the living area, barely able to move from the huge amounts of food consumed. 'We really should learn to eat less!' my aunt would exclaim. For a brief moment I would agree but then my greed would overtake me and I would respond by saying that we hadn't eaten all that much really. The other members of my family would look towards me with grins of appreciation.

This wonderful family tradition continues to this day and I feel very lucky to be a part of it. Unfortunately my uncle passed away some years ago and I dearly miss our conversations. I often imagine him sitting next to me in the now empty chair, still racing to eat his meal. I look over to him and smile approvingly.

Baklava

Baklava is traditionally made with layers of filo pastry filled with chopped almonds, walnuts or pistachios and spices, then sweetened with sugar syrup or honey. I prefer to use honey, as was used in ancient times, and you can use any combination of nuts to suit your taste. This sticky treat is delicious on its own, or serve it with ice-cream or honeyed Greek-style yoghurt. Another wonderful way to enjoy it is to crush leftover *baklava* and fold it through vanilla ice-cream.

200 g finely chopped almonds
200 g finely chopped walnuts
3 tablespoons breadcrumbs
3 tablespoons castor sugar
2 tablespoons ground
   cinnamon
1–2 teaspoons ground cloves
200 g unsalted butter, melted
20 sheets filo pastry
375 g thyme-infused honey

Makes 12 pieces

Preheat the oven to 160°C.

Combine the nuts, breadcrumbs, sugar and spices in a bowl and mix well.

Brush a baking dish with melted butter and line the base with two sheets of filo pastry. Brush generously with butter. Top with two more sheets of pastry and brush again. Repeat with another two sheets of pastry (cover the remaining sheets with a tea towel to prevent them drying out).

Sprinkle some of the nut mixture evenly over the pastry. Place two sheets of filo over the nut mixture and brush the top sheet generously with butter. Continue layering until you are left with four sheets of filo on the top. Brush lightly with the remaining butter.

Score the top layer of pastry into 12 diamond or square pieces. Sprinkle with a little water and bake for 45 minutes or until golden brown.

About 10 minutes before the *baklava* is due to come out of the oven, place the honey in a small saucepan over medium heat. When it just begins to simmer take the pan off the heat and allow the honey to cool for 5 minutes.

Pour the honey syrup evenly over the *baklava*, then leave to stand for at least 15 minutes so the pastry soaks up the syrup. Cut into pieces and serve.

Greek yoghurt cake with ouzo and lemon syrup >

This is my aunt Stavroula's recipe, but I have spiked it with some *ouzo* (this is optional – if you leave it out, increase the water to 1 cup).

65 g unsalted butter,
   at room temperature
1 cup sugar
5 eggs
300 g Greek-style yoghurt
2½ cups self-raising flour,
   sifted
1 teaspoon baking powder,
   sifted

Syrup
1 cup water
½ cup *ouzo*
juice of 1 lemon
zest of 1 lemon, extremely
   thinly sliced
2 cups castor sugar

Serves 10–12

Preheat the oven to 180°C and grease a 20 cm cake tin.

Beat the butter and sugar in an electric mixer until pale and creamy, then add the eggs one by one, beating constantly. Add the yoghurt, flour and baking powder and continue to beat until the mixture forms a smooth batter.

Pour the batter into the prepared tin and bake for 1 hour or until the cake is risen and golden brown (a skewer inserted into the centre should come out clean). Turn out onto a wire rack and leave to cool completely.

To make the syrup, combine the water, *ouzo* (if using), lemon juice, lemon zest and sugar in a saucepan and bring to the boil. Reduce the heat to low and simmer until the liquid has reduced and thickened to a syrup.

Cut the cake into pieces. Pour the syrup over the cake and let it soak in for about 10 minutes before serving.

Baked apples with commandaria

Commandaria is a honey-sweet red wine that is also used in Greek Orthodox churches for Holy Communion. It dates back at least two thousand years and was previously called *mana*, the Greek word for 'mother'. If you can't find it, use port or muscat.

8 red apples
3 tablespoons slivered
   almonds, toasted
3 tablespoons dry currants
   or sultanas
4 tablespoons castor sugar
40 g unsalted butter
1 cup *commandaria*
1 cinnamon stick
½ teaspoon ground cinnamon
½ teaspoon ground nutmeg
½ teaspoon ground cloves

Serves 4

Preheat the oven to 150°C. Wash and core the apples and place in a baking dish. Stuff the hollows with the almonds and currants or sultanas, followed by ½ teaspoon sugar and 1 teaspoon butter in each apple. Pour a little of the *commandaria* into each hollow, then pour the rest around the apples together with 2–3 tablespoons water.

Add the cinnamon stick to the dish and sprinkle the ground spices over the apples. Cover the dish with foil and bake the apples for 35 minutes. Remove the foil, increase the oven temperature to 180°C and bake for a further 5–10 minutes until the apples are golden. Serve with Greek-style yoghurt or ice-cream.

Mastic ricotta cakes with fresh figs poached in mavrodaphne

In this recipe I poach the figs in a red dessert wine called *mavrodaphne*, which comes from Patra. You can use port instead, if you wish. During the winter months I replace the figs with quinces, and when they are in season I love to use cherries.

2 tablespoons mastic liqueur
   or other liqueur (optional)
3 tablespoons currants
½ cup dry-roasted almonds
2 cups fresh ricotta
2 tablespoons honey
   (I use thyme-infused
   honey from Crete)
2 teaspoons ground cinnamon
1–2 tablespoons semolina
1 tablespoon chopped mint
1 teaspoon ground cinnamon,
   extra, to garnish

Poached figs
8 fresh figs
1 cup *mavrodaphne*
1 cinnamon stick
4 cloves
3 tablespoons castor sugar

Serves 4

If you are using liqueur, place the currants and liqueur in a small bowl, cover and set aside for at least 1 hour.

Use a mortar and pestle to roughly grind the almonds – they should be coarsely textured, not ground to a powder.

Place the ricotta, honey, cinnamon, semolina and ground almonds in a bowl, add the currants and liqueur (if using) and mix gently to combine. Cover and refrigerate for at least 2 hours.

Preheat the oven to 180°C.

To make the poached figs, combine the figs, *mavrodaphne*, cinnamon stick and cloves in a saucepan and bring to the boil. Reduce the heat to low and simmer for 20 minutes.

Meanwhile, divide the ricotta mixture among four small baking tins (or spoon the mixture into four muffin moulds, to about three-quarters full). Bake for 15–20 minutes until the tops are lightly golden. Remove from the oven and set aside to cool slightly – you want to serve them warm.

Remove the figs from the pan and add the sugar to the remaining poaching liquid. Cook for a couple of minutes until the liquid thickens slightly, then remove the pan from the heat.

Place one ricotta cake and two figs on each serving plate. Garnish with mint and cinnamon, and drizzle with the poaching liquid.

The going-away gathering that my mother had with friends and family in Kalamata, in 1959, shortly before leaving for Australia

My mother in her new home in Darlinghurst, Sydney

While living in Kalamata, my mother (right), like her sister, started work from a very young age to help support the family. My mother sewed women's clothing and my aunt was a tailor.

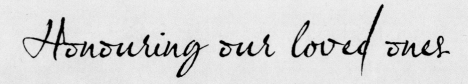

Honouring our loved ones

Unlike other Greek families, my family here in Australia is quite small. I have my aunt Stavroula, my sister Katina and three cousins, Manny, Chris and Con. Many members of our extended family still live on the islands of Greece, but tragedy has kept our family in Australia small. My grandmother Amalia and her son Panagioti were both killed in a car accident soon after migrating to Australia, on 17 October 1965. Panagioti was only 33. Eight years later, on 3 November 1973, while my sister and I were living on the island of Psara, my mother lost her battle with cancer. She was also 33. These were very difficult years for my aunt Stavroula because she had essentially lost all her extended family in Australia. I sometimes wonder how things would have been if my ancestors had not left Greece.

I believe that it is my family's strong faith in the Greek Orthodox religion that gave us all the courage, strength and will to overcome these losses and to move forward with our lives. Cooking my grandmother Amalia's recipes, which were passed down to my aunt and then on to me, has also been important as it has served to connect us with our loved ones.

I recall our regular visits to the cemetery when I was a teenager. It's a ritual that continues to this day. For our family the cemetery is an extension of our home. We visit on special days, including name days, Easter and Christmas, and of course on anniversaries. We spend many hours cleaning the graves of our departed family members, arranging fresh flowers and lighting the *kantilia*, or lanterns. We burn some *livani* (incense made from frankincense, used specifically for religious purposes) and say a special prayer. Prior to Christmas we adorn the graves with decorations and in this way include our loved ones in our celebrations.

During these visits to the cemetery we spend time reflecting on the happy moments we all spent together. We feel the presence of our departed loved ones and the visit provides us with a sense of inner peace and happiness.

On some days we make *kolliva* (see recipe over the page) and take this to the cemetery. This is a special sweet wheat dish that is made to commemorate the dead. Wheat is first boiled then mixed with sugar and raisins and decorated with pomegranate seeds. The pomegranate is very important as it is an offering to those loved ones who have left us in this world and whom we will rejoin in the next life. It symbolises the resurrection, as well as the sweetness and abundance of life.

My aunt makes *kolliva* on the anniversary of my mother's death and at other special times of the year, and we take it to the cemetery. The priest then performs a special liturgy and we distribute the *kolliva* to everyone there. The people who consume the *kolliva* will usually say a few words of prayer for the dearly departed before they eat it. This ritual of distributing the *kolliva* at the cemetery connects us with other people whom we know as well as strangers who have had a similar loss. They share their stories and pain with us and tell us whom they have come to visit. We reciprocate and share ours.

Preparing *kolliva* is not only a tradition but is also a great way to help mend the wounds in the heart of everyone who has lost a loved one. In this way, we keep alive the spirit of our loved ones and remember the wonderful moments we spent together.

We also honour our loved ones throughout the year with memorial services known as *mnimosyma*. At Easter and on All Souls' Day (*psihosavato*), the names of the deceased are read aloud in church. Again we prepare *kolliva*, which is then blessed by the priest and given out to the congregation in memory of the deceased.

Kolliva

When we Greeks commemorate our dead we make *kolliva*, a tradition that helps to heal the heart and keep alive the spirit of our loved ones. I have used cinnamon here, but you could use cumin instead.

500 g wheat kernels
2 teaspoons ground cinnamon, plus extra, for decorating
250 g walnuts, chopped
½ cup raisins
250 g sesame seeds, toasted and crushed
½ cup icing sugar, sifted
½ cup blanched almonds, halved
seeds of 1 pomegranate

Serves 4–6

Cover the wheat kernels with water and soak overnight. Drain and rinse well.

Fill a saucepan with water, add the soaked wheat and bring to a rapid boil. Reduce the heat and simmer for 2 hours until the wheat is tender and begins to split open. Stir frequently to prevent sticking, and add more water as required. When the wheat is cooked, remove the pan from the heat and leave to stand for about 30 minutes.

Drain the wheat and rinse thoroughly in a colander. Spread it out on a clean tea towel and leave for about 2 hours, shaking occasionally. Place in a bowl, add the cinnamon, walnuts, raisins and half the sesame seeds and mix gently.

Press the mixture down hard on a serving platter and spread the remaining sesame seeds evenly over the top. Dust with a thin layer of icing sugar.

Sprinkle the cinnamon to form a cross on the *kolliva*, then place the almonds on either side of the cinnamon to follow the cross. Place the pomegranate seeds over the exposed icing sugar to form a colourful design.

To serve, simply spoon some of the mixture into small bowls. Serve at room temperature.

Yoghurt with pomegranate, honey and cinnamon >

This is very quick and easy to make, yet is sure to impress. The key is to use good-quality ingredients – I like to use thyme-infused honey from Crete or Psara.

1 pomegranate
250 g Greek-style yoghurt
1–2 tablespoons honey, plus extra, for drizzling
1–2 teaspoons ground cinnamon

Makes about 1 cup

Carefully remove the seeds from the pomegranate and place in a bowl. Save 1 tablespoon of the seeds to use as a garnish.

Add the remaining ingredients to the bowl and mix well, squashing some of the pomegranate seeds to release their juices as you go. Decorate with the reserved pomegranate seeds and a drizzle of honey and serve.

Saffron rizogalo with cinnamon spun sugar

Rizogalo is a traditional rice-pudding dessert, served warm or at room temperature. I have added my spin to the traditional recipe by incorporating other ingredients I'm passionate about, such as rosewater and saffron. The spun sugar is a whimsical touch that makes the dish visually spectacular, but of course you can serve the pudding without it.

4 cups milk
½ teaspoon saffron threads
½ cup short-grain or
    arborio rice
4 tablespoons castor sugar
½ cup currants
1 tablespoon grated
    orange zest
1 teaspoon rosewater
2 egg yolks, beaten
ground cinnamon, to serve

Spun sugar
300 ml water
300 g castor sugar
½–1 teaspoon ground
    cinnamon
olive oil, for greasing

Serves 4

Pour the milk into a saucepan over medium heat and bring to a simmer. Reduce the heat to a slow simmer and stir in the saffron, rice and sugar, then add the currants and orange zest. Simmer, stirring regularly, for 40–45 minutes until thick and creamy. A couple of minutes before the end of the cooking time, add the rosewater and egg and mix well.

While the *rizogalo* is cooking, prepare the spun sugar (alternatively, you can prepare this in advance and keep it in a cool place).

Combine the water, sugar and cinnamon in a saucepan over medium heat and stir until the sugar has dissolved. Bring to the boil, then reduce the heat and cook for about 5 minutes until the mixture becomes a thick golden caramel. Remove from the heat.

Line a flat tray with baking paper and rub olive oil over two rolling pins. Place the rolling pins on the tray, a little apart. Dip a fork in the caramel mixture and wave it up and down the tray over the rolling pins so that the caramel forms fine strands. Repeat until you have used all the caramel mixture. You can mould the spun sugar strands into balls or whatever shape you like. Alternatively, simply break off some strands.

Spoon the *rizogalo* into serving bowls, leave to cool slightly then sprinkle with cinnamon. Top with some of the spun sugar and serve.

Frappe

Frappe (iced Greek coffee) is not just a drink, it's a way of life. It is almost compulsory to sit at least once a day outside a café, very slowly sipping your *frappe* as you watch the world go by. It's a time to relax and talk about anything and everything.

When you place your order, you must always specify whether you would like your coffee *sketo*, *metrio* or *gliko*, which indicates the amount of sugar you want added: *sketo* = no sugar, *metrio* = 2 teaspoons sugar, and *gliko* = 3 teaspoons sugar. I often add honey rather than sugar, and you could also use soy milk instead of regular milk if you prefer.

1 cup cold water
  (from the fridge)
ice cubes
1–1½ teaspoons instant coffee
sugar, to taste
milk, to taste

Serves 1

In a long glass or *frappe* container (similar to a cocktail shaker) place 2 tablespoons cold water, 2 ice cubes, the coffee and sugar. Shake in the *frappe* container or use a small hand-held blender to mix until it foams.

Pour into a tall glass. Half-fill the glass with ice cubes and top up with water and milk. Drink with a straw.

< Greek coffee

I cannot start the day without a cup of Greek coffee. I make it in a *briki* (see picture opposite), which is a tall, narrow implement with a long handle and a lip, usually made out of copper, aluminium or stainless steel. You could use a very small saucepan instead, but you may not achieve the froth on top. Sometimes I add a dash of *ouzo* or grind a piece of *masticha* crystal with a teaspoon of sugar and add this when the coffee is beginning to bubble.

cold water
1–1½ teaspoons Greek coffee
sugar, to taste

Serves 1

Fill a cup with cold water and pour this into the *briki*. Add the coffee and sugar and stir over low heat until the coffee and sugar dissolve.

Hold the *briki* by the handle as it comes to the boil. When it starts to foam, let it rise until it almost reaches the lip of the *briki* then immediately take it off the heat so it doesn't spill everywhere.

Let the coffee stand for a few seconds and then pour into the cup. If you are making coffee for more than one person, pour a little into each cup first to distribute the froth evenly, then fill the cups to the top.

Serve with a glass of cold water and drink it slowly.

Glossary of ingredients

While some of these ingredients so key to Greek cooking can be found in the supermarket (such as filo, feta and Greek yoghurt), almost all can be found in a good continental deli. The exceptions, of course, are ouzo *and mastic liqueur, which you will need to hunt down in the bottle shop, and sea urchin, which you may have to order from your local seafood supplier.*

Avgotaracho
The orange-coloured roe of mullet is pressed, smoked and encased in beeswax to make *avgotaracho*. It has a caramelised salt-fish flavour. A Greek delicacy, it is eaten as is with lemon juice, or in Greek savoury dishes.

Barley rusks
A specialty of Crete, rusks or *paximathia* are thick slices of bread that are twice-baked until hard and crisp. I love to serve them with dips or as part of a *meze* plate.

Capers and caper leaves
The Greeks love capers and the leaves of the caper plant. In late spring and early summer, it is not unusual to see capers hanging over rocks all over the Greek islands, especially in gorgeous Santorini. If you buy them packed in salt, they need rinsing and draining before use, but if you buy them in brine they just need draining. In Greece, the leaves are often boiled with other wild greens and dressed with olive oil and lemon juice, or we pickle them and serve them in salads.

Feta
Feta is the best-known of the Greek cheeses – a hard, salty cheese, usually made from goat or sheep's milk. See pages 76–7 for more on this wonderful cheese.

Filo
Filo is a thin pastry used to make sweet and savoury pies and sweets. It also comes in shredded form, known as *kataifi*. When a recipe asks you to cut the pastry into lengths, I find it easiest to cut while the pastry is still rolled up, then unroll and proceed with the recipe. As a general rule, brush it with olive oil in savoury dishes and butter in sweet dishes.

Graviera
Graviera is a traditional Greek cheese manufactured exclusively in Crete. Made from ewe or sheep's milk or a combination of both, as well as small quantities of goat's milk, it is hard cheese with a slightly sweet flavour. It can be enjoyed grated or fried, or simply served as a *meze* drizzled with a little honey.

Haloumi

This wonderful salty cheese originated in Cyprus. Traditionally made from a mixture of goat and sheep's milk, it holds its shape when fried and is often garnished with mint or lemon. For the best texture, serve it warm.

Kasseri

This creamy gold-coloured cheese is made from sheep or goat's milk. It melts well and is great for grilling, grating or to accompany a fruit platter.

Kataifi *see* Filo

Kefalograviera

Made of sheep and cow's milk, this cheese has a mild nutty flavour with salty undertones. It is commonly used in pies or grated over pasta. At weddings in Crete they drizzle it (or *graviera* cheese) with honey and offer it to their guests. As with feta, Greece has been granted a protected designation of origin (PDO) status for this cheese. Beware inferior-quality copies from Germany and Austria. They are not worth the cost.

Kefalotiri

A hard, mildly salty cheese made of goat or sheep's milk, used in the same way as you would *kefalograviera*. I believe Greek authorities are in the process of achieving a PDO status for this traditional cheese. As with *kefalograviera*, beware of imitation cheeses not made in Greece.

Mahlepi

This aromatic spice comes from the seeds of the St Lucie Cherry. It has a distinctive fruity taste with tones of bitter almonds and is used in Greece for holiday cakes such as *tsoureki* (see page 140).

Masticha

The *masticha* or mastic tree is a type of gum that produces an almost clear crystal edible substance. It grows in only one place in the world: the island of Chios. The sweet flavour is unique and therefore hard to describe, but it is most often ground with flour or sugar and added to biscuits, cakes, ice-cream and spoon sweets. It is also used in savoury dishes. *Masticha* is one of my most treasured ingredients, and I use it in many dishes because of its healing and therapeutic properties.

Mastic liqueur

Also produced is Chios, this is a sweet liqueur flavoured with mastic (see above).

Myzithra

In Greece *myzithra* cheese comes in many forms and varies in flavour from sweet to sour or salty. It can have a soft ricotta-like texture, or can come in a harder form. In Australia we have the hard form made from sheep's milk. Serve it on its own, grated over pasta or use it in pies.

Olive oil

To the Greeks, the olive tree is a symbol of knowledge, wisdom, abundance, peace, strength, beauty and health and its produce is essential in our cuisine. Most regions produce award-winning olive oil; in fact, Greek olive oil is so good that some Italian producers purchase it from Greece, re-label it and sell it as Italian! It is believed that the first cultivation of olive trees ocurred in Crete during the Minoan civilisation. This is one of the reasons I love using olive oil from Crete. Look for deep golden or a dark green extra virgin olive oil with fresh grassy or fruity aromas.

Ouzo

Ouzo is a spirit made from the distilled residue of grapes, with anise and herbal flavouring added during production. It turns cloudy when water is added. The European Union recently backed Greece's request to continue trade protection of *ouzo* as exclusively Greek.

Pastourma

This is a pungent, spicy cured beef and is usually rubbed with flavourings such as cumin and fenugreek. It can be lightly baked and tossed in salads, used in stuffings or simply eaten as is with cheese and figs on hot crusty bread.

Saffron

Saffron threads are the dried stigmas of the saffron flower and must be picked by hand, making it the most expensive spice in the world. It was considered by Hippocrates to be an excellent stomach ailment and antispasmodic. The saffron I use is cultivated in the area of Kozani, in Macedonia. It has the most beautiful and vibrant deep red colour and the floral flavour is very pronounced.

Sea urchin

Sea urchins are small, spiny sea creatures found in many parts of Greece. Inside, they contain the most wonderful vibrant orange roe, which is used in savoury dishes or served raw with a little salt and lemon juice.

Tarama

Tarama is sea-mullet fish roe. Considered a Greek delicacy it is used to make *taramosalata* (see page 38).

Vine leaves

Vine leaves are used to wrap up fillings, such as in the signature Greek dish *dolmades* (see page 61). You can purchase vine leaves in brine or dried and salted, but the best way to have them is fresh off the vine. Look to see if one of your neighbours has a grapevine in their backyard or, better yet, plant your own. Remember to pick just the young and tender ones. If you are using leaves from a packet, rinse them first to remove most of saltiness.

Yeast

Although it comes in fresh or dried form, I tend to use dry yeast because it does not require refrigeration and has a longer shelf life than fresh yeast. As with all baking ingredients, make sure you measure it correctly.

Yoghurt

Thick, strained yoghurt is an essential part of Greek cooking. Greek yoghurts are made with either goat, sheep or cow's milk, and are used in both savoury dishes and sweets, including the famous Greek yoghurt cake drizzled with lemon syrup (see page 196).

Index

LANTERN

Published by the Penguin Group
Penguin Group (Australia)
250 Camberwell Road, Camberwell, Victoria 3124, Australia
(a division of Pearson Australia Group Pty Ltd)
Penguin Group (USA) Inc.
375 Hudson Street, New York, New York 10014, USA
Penguin Group (Canada)
90 Eglinton Avenue East, Suite 700, Toronto, Canada ON M4P 2Y3
(a division of Pearson Penguin Canada Inc.)
Penguin Books Ltd
80 Strand, London WC2R 0RL England
Penguin Ireland
25 St Stephen's Green, Dublin 2, Ireland
(a division of Penguin Books Ltd)
Penguin Books India Pvt Ltd
11 Community Centre, Panchsheel Park, New Delhi – 110 017, India
Penguin Group (NZ)
67 Apollo Drive, Rosedale, North Shore 0632, New Zealand
(a division of Pearson New Zealand Ltd)
Penguin Books (South Africa) (Pty) Ltd
24 Sturdee Avenue, Rosebank, Johannesburg 2196, South Africa

Penguin Books Ltd, Registered Offices: 80 Strand, London,
  WC2R 0RL, England

First published by Penguin Group (Australia), 2009

10 9 8 7 6 5 4 3 2 1

Design by Danie Pout Design © Penguin Group (Australia)
Photography by Alan Benson
Styling by Michelle Noerianto
Typeset in Aldine 721 BT by Post Pre-Press Group,
  Brisbane, Queensland
Colour reproduction by Splitting Image Colour Studio Pty Ltd,
  Clayton, Victoria
Printed and bound in Singapore by Imago Productions

Quotation from *The Colossus of Maroussi* on pages 176–7 reproduced
with permission of Curtis Brown Group Ltd, London on behalf of
the Estate of Henry Miller © Henry Miller 1941.

National Library of Australia
Cataloguing-in-Publication data:

Benardis, Maria.

My Greek table / Maria Benardis;
photography by Alan Benson

978 192 138216 1 (hbk.)

Includes index.
Cookery, Greek.

641.59495

penguin.com.au

Acknowledgements

I am thankful and grateful to God, the Virgin Mary (whom I am
named after) and Saint Fanourios for guiding me and setting
me on this new path.

This book would not have being possible without my aunt
Stavroula Kargas, who has taught me everything I know about
cooking high-quality traditional Greek dishes. Thank you
for always being there to share your stories, for your support
and most importantly your love.

A heartfelt thank you to Mrs Katzenos, Mrs Michaelides and
Mrs Poulopoulos for sharing their wonderful recipes and stories.
They are a true testament to the fact that you can get through
any hardship or problem that life throws your way.

Thank you for coming into my life Amber Forrest-Bisley.
I appreciate all the support with the PR for Greekalicious.
I consider you a part of my family. Thank you also to the rest
of the Cardinal Spin team.

To my friends Sylvain Roy and Phillip McGrath, I need pages
to express my gratitude. Thank you for always being there when
I need you and for listening. Your loyalty and love is deeply
appreciated. Phillip, thank you for your wonderful work with
the Greekalicious website and with the food photography.

To my treasured friend and mentor, Sharyn Grant, thank you
for your understanding and spiritual guidance. I could not
have made the Greekalicious dream possible without you.

To my agent Selwa Anthony, thank you for believing in me.

Thank you to the wonderful team at Penguin – Julie Gibbs,
Ingrid Ohlsson, Jane Morrow and Rachel Carter – for believing
in me and in my vision. Thank you for your professionalism,
wonderful work and passion. And to designer Danie Pout,
thanks for making this such a beautiful book to look at.

Alan Benson, you are an unbelievably talented photographer.
Michelle Noerianto, your styling was amazing and captured
everything I dreamt. Thank you both for working on the book
and for bringing the dishes to life.

I also wanted to extend a special thank you to Greece and its
people for their generosity and willingness to share their stories,
culture, traditions, recipes, hospitality and love whenever I am
there. This book is for all the Greeks all over the world. You are
so fortunate to be a part of a civilisation that has contributed
many things to this world including gastronomy.